Chicagoland Trail Guide

by Eileen Kelley

Publisher
Eliot R. Wineberg

This book is dedicated to
SETH DANIEL

In Gratitude

Warmest thanks to my mentors and former employers, Edwin Scott and Diane Wilson Everett, for leading me by the hand through the publishing process; Forest Preserve Districts and representatives in the counties of Kane, Lake, McHenry, Cook, Will, and DuPage - my respect for your work continues to grow; Frank Rich of Rails-to-Trails for believing in my work; Nancy Kaymen of the Chicago Park District for the copious information I am unable to adequately relate on the Lakefront Trail; Mary Thorne of Windy City Sports Magazine and Rex Quinn of Quinn Publishers for their support and promotion of this work; Susan Pinsof of Northeastern Illinois Planning Commission; Keith Mistrik and Larry O'Toole of the Chicago Area Bicycle Dealers Association; and Randy Newfeld of the Chicagoland Bicycle Federation for your invaluable knowledge and direction; Friends and Family who have encouraged me from the moment the spark entered my mind; and lastly, my publisher, Eliot Wineberg, for the ultimate gift of faith...betting HIS time and money on my effort.

Printed in the United States of America
ISBN 0-9639686-0-2 $10.95

If you have any questions or comments concerning this book, please write:

Chicagoland Trail Guide
c/o The Amateur Athlete
7840 N. Lincoln Ave., Suite 204
Skokie, IL. 60077

Contents

Trail Summary

Cook County Trails

Kane County Trails

Lake County Trails

Introduction

In May of 1991, I strolled into a book shop to pick up a gift for my husband, Vince, for Father's Day. The avid bicycler that he is, I looked for an off-road bicycle trail book for the greater Chicagoland area — a book that would provide places for biking and be within 60 miles of Chicago. I visualized "Himself" coming home from work, loading his bike in the van and unwinding on a nearby trail. I learned that such a book did not exist. The idea occurred to me that if I wanted such a book, maybe I should write one.

In the summer of 1991, I took a three month sabbatical from work and rode over 50 trails in the area. I began my quest riding two to seven mile trails (1 hour) and worked up to 25 miles (4 hours). By the end of summer, I awoke one morning to discover my quads were preventing me from rolling over. What a shock!

The result of my efforts is the most complete compilation of Chicago area cycle and ski trails available. I have endeavored to provide thorough and consistent information about each and every trail. I made a concerted effort NOT to include trails that would infringe on the privacy of homeowners (i.e., housing development trails). I invite you, the reader, to contribute additional facts and to suggest categories you would like included in future editions of this guidebook. Many of the users of this trail guide will load their bikes or skis onto the family car and travel some distance to explore trails that they have never seen. With that in mind, I have attempted to let users know what to expect when they get to the trail they have chosen to explore.

In addition to information about directions, trail head parking and facilities, I have added my own comments about most of the trails. My opinions may not match yours, but I hope to give you an idea about the nature of the trail so that you do not find a trail that is "urban" when you wanted "country" — or find flat farmland when you are looking for hills.

If you have treated yourself to the purchase of this trail guide, treat yourself to something even more rewarding. The exercise you will get will obviously benefit your body. But your spirit will benefit from being outdoors and enjoying the many sights and sounds, both man-made and natural. Being a Southeastern U.S. native, I'm accustomed to mountains and oceans at my back door. Chicago has not met my East Coast memories of geographical variety and beauty. After riding these trails this past year, I've expanded my limited view of Illinois terrain. I wish I had enjoyed the natural beauty of these trails and forest preserves a long time ago. My hope is that you will discover the variety of nature Chicagoland has to offer.

Safety

In this guide, identified are the dangerous road crossings that you will encounter. It is easy to get careless, however, when you are rolling along on a trail and forget frequent crossings at side streets. It may sound silly to say, but on such trails people often forget to slow down and look both ways.

The following RULES OF TRAIL RIDING will improve your chances of having a safe ride:

- Always ride on the right side of the trail.
- When there is a lot of traffic, ride single file rather than side by side. Think about how you feel when you have riders coming at you side by side — hogging the whole trail.
- When riding with kids, you have to frequently remind them about staying to the right. They easily get distracted and forget.
- When passing, always announce yourself by saying "Passing on your left" or simply "on your left." This alerts the jogger or rider ahead of you and reduces the chance that they will make an unexpected move in front of you.
- Wear a helmet! The most serious injury one can suffer on a bicycle is a head injury. Wearing a helmet dramatically reduces that risk. At $30 to $60, they may seem like a luxury you can't afford. If you ever had an accident, you would gladly have paid ten times the price. Most people will never have a need for one, but then most people will never need their seat belts either. Besides, you'll look more like you belong when you wear a helmet on a bike trail.

Bicycles & Equipment

The trails in this guide can be enjoyed on a used Huffy bike from a garage sale or an $8,000 custom built 24 speed racing model (Yes, you CAN spend that much on a bike!). The mountain bike has been a very popular seller in the past few years. It has fatter tires and more upright seating than the old standard 10-speed. These bikes are designed for off-road cycling. The fat tires will dig through mud and rock while skinny tire bikes would become bogged down. The upright riding position feels more confortable to many riders.

Most bicycles come with three sets of chain rings (the cogs in the front where the pedals are) and six or seven rings on the freewheel (the cogs on the rear wheel). Multiplying six times three results in eighteen speeds. Actually many of these speeds overlap. Why so many then? The small chain ring on front in combination with the large chain ring in the rear will allow you to climb very steep hills with minimal effort. The combination of large in front and small in rear requires maximum effort,but rcsults in the highest speed per revolution of the pedals. With all of these advantages, why should anyone purchase one of those drop handlebar skinny tire bikes? (They are known as tour bikes, road bikes or racers.) The fact is that they are much faster and really do ride much better on hard pavement. The big tires on mountain bikes create a lot more rolling resistance on smooth surfaces. That means a lot more work to go the same distance or speed as a road bike. The upright riding position also creates a lot more wind resistance.

A modified version of the mountain bike has been developed. It is usually called a cross bike and has tires which are about 1-3/8'' wide compared to 1½'' or 2'' on a mountain bike and 1'' to 1¼'' on a road bike. If you are thinking about buying a new bike, think about the kind of riding that you do. If you ride short distances around town and sometimes on trails, a cross bike is probably your best bet. If you really want to get away from it all and like to ride trails which most people would only think of hiking, then consider a mountain bike. If your preference is for a mix of road and paved trails, yet speed and distance are important, then nothing will satisfy you like a road bike.

HOW MUCH SHOULD YOU SPEND? Most bikes are ridden less than 500 miles in their lifetime. If that will be true of your next bike, spend accordingly. In general, the more you spend on equipment, the better it will serve you. If you plan to ride a lot, then good equipment is worth the investment. When it comes to getting good equipment, a reputable bike shop with knowledgeable sales people and sufficient inventory is the only place to shop. You will get comparable features and quality for a comparable amount of money spent. So shop for a dealer you like and trust rather than trying to simply shop for a deal.

Bicycle Accessories

Hip Bags (fanny packs):

A worth-while investment. Men, women and children use them. They're convenient for carrying maps, money, emergency change for phone calls, bike repair tools, food, car keys and of course, your bike trail guide.

Spare tire, bicycle pump, water bottle:

If you carry a spare tube you will not need to REPAIR one on the trail. Take this author's word for that hard-learned tip. Take the bad one off, tuck it away in your fanny pack, insert the new one, pump it with your bicycle pump (which attaches to your bicycle frame) and be on your way. You can patch at home in your spare (pun) time. Invest in a good water bottle. Fill it up (partially) and freeze it overnight. Wrap it in a cooler cup before you leave (if you are driving to a trail). By the time you hit the trail, you will still have COOL water to drink. Some of the indicated water pumps/fountains are inoperable at times. It is best to rely on your own water supply.

Skis

If you are a novice to cross country skiing, it might be best to obtain a book on the subject. It is a very easy sport to learn and the equipment needs are minimal. Ski packages, which include skis, bindings, shoes and poles are often sold at sporting goods stores for less than $150. The only additional equipment you need is warm clothes. Rental equipment is available at a number of bicycle and ski shops. It is also available at DuPage County's Blackwell Forest Preserve when there is snow on the ground. This is a good way to find out whether or not you will like this sport.

Cross country skiing has developed into two distinct styles in recent years. The traditional style has the skier SLIDING his feet in a more or less fore and back movement. If you watch the winter Olympics, you will see the cross country ski racers using a SKATING style. This is much faster, but also requires a much higher energy level. The skis used for these two styles are different from one another. The ones usually found at rental locations and those most used by the average skiing population are the traditional fore and aft skis. Unless you are more aggressive and energetic in your athletic pursuits, the traditional skis are probably the best choice for beginners.

Clothing

Both cycling and skiing build up a lot of body heat. Freedom of motion is also important in both sports. For that reason, specialized clothing has been developed. Lycra — which may look or feel a little strange, really makes riding or skiing easier. It protects from the wind and stretches in every direction. While denim may have been popular for years, it serves you poorly when you want your legs to move freely without building up a lot of perspiration. You don't have to invest in a whole new wardrobe just to take a bike ride or go skiing now and then. Just remember that you want to wear what works with your body and not against it. Most of that strange looking clothing you see in the bike and ski shops is very functional.

The Safety, Bicycles & Equipment, Skis and Clothing sections were prepared by Vince Kelley. I want to credit my husband for riding and documenting many of the trails with me and for me.

LEGEND

 PICNIC GROUNDS

 TELEPHONES

 FOOD LOCATIONS

 SHOPPING CENTERS

 RAILROAD CROSSING

 SECURITY OFFICE

 OVERNIGHT ACCOMODATIONS

 POINTS OF INTEREST

 BICYCLE MAINTENANCE

 PLAYGROUNDS

 VEHICLE PARKING

 HIGHWAY CROSSING

 BICYCLE RACKS

 FIRST AID

 WATER

 DANGEROUS CROSSING

 RESTROOMS

 TRAIL

Cook County Trails

Arie Crown
Bemis Woods
Busse Woods
Chicago Lakefront
Deer Grove
Evanston-Chicago Connection
Evanston-Lakeshore
Green Bay Trail
I & M Canal
Illinois Prairie Path
North Branch
North Shore Channel
Palatine Trail
Thorn Creek
Tinley Creek

According to the Cook County Forest
Preserve District, water, restrooms and
picnic tables are located near parking lots
in all Cook County Forest Preserves.

Arie Crown
Forest Trail

Trail Distance . . . . 3.2 Miles
Trail Surface . . . . Packed Dirt
Type of Use . . . . Mountain
Towns . . . . Countryside,
Hodgkins, Willow Springs,
Indian Head Park
. . . . Cook

County . . . .

Author's Comments: This is a series of interconnected bumpy dirt trails through fairly dense woods. They are not well marked and it is easy to become disoriented. However, they frequently cross the road which loops through the preserve. On two visits here I noticed a large population of single men cruising the area. Ride this one with a companion.

For Detailed Information
Forest Preserve District of Cook County
536 N. Harlem Ave.
River Forest, IL 60305   708-366-9420

For Calendar of Events
in Surrounding Communities
LaGrange West Suburban
Chamber of Commerce
Peter Solie, Executive Director
512 W. Burlington Ave., P.O. Box 187
LaGrange, IL 60525   708-352-0494

Directions for parking: I-55 to Rt. 45, north .25 miles to the entrance on the west side. Approximately nine to ten parking lots exist alongside the preserve road.

Bemis Woods Trail (Salt Creek)

Trail Distance . . . . 6.6 Miles
Trail Surface . . . . Paved
Type of Use . . . . Tour
Towns . . . . Western Springs,
LaGrange Park, Westchester,
Brookfield
County . . . . Cook

Author's Comments: The variety of hills, sinkholes, prairies, geology, fauna and flora make this trail one of the best in Chicagoland. This trail is worth the effort despite the numerous, stressful road crossings.

For Detailed Information
Forest Preserve District of Cook County
536 N. Harlem Ave.
River Forest, IL 60305   708-366-9420

NIPC
400 W. Madison St.
Chicago, IL 60606   312-454-0400

For Calendar of Events
in Surrounding Communities
Westchester Village Hall
10240 Roosevelt Rd.
Westchester, IL 60514   708-345-0020

Westchester Chamber of Commerce
Dr. Thomas Sullivan, Pres.
P.O. Box 7309
Westchester, IL 60514   708-562-7747

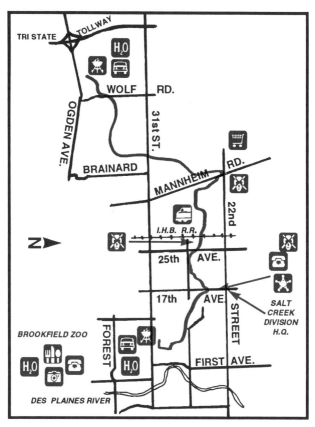

Directions for parking: West Trailhead: 294 exit east on Ogden Ave. (Rt. 34). Turn north at Bemis Woods South Entrance. Trailhead begins on east side of entrance road.

East Trailhead: 294 turn east on Ogden Ave. Turn north on 1st Ave., west on 31st and park.

Brookfield Chamber of Commerce
Florence Rooney, Sec.
3724 Grand Blvd.
Brookfield, IL 60513   708-485-1434

LaGrange West Suburban
Chamber of Commerce
Peter Solie, Exec. Dir.
512 W. Burlington Ave.
LaGrange, IL 60525   708-352-0494

Busse Woods Trail

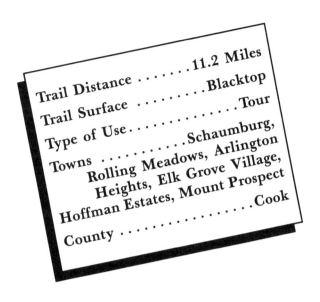

Trail Distance . . . . 11.2 Miles
Trail Surface . . . . Blacktop
Type of Use . . . . Tour
Towns . . . . Schaumburg, Rolling Meadows, Arlington Heights, Elk Grove Village, Hoffman Estates, Mount Prospect
County . . . . Cook

Author's Comments: This trail is so popular on summer weekends with joggers, in-line skaters and bikers that the 12 MPH speed limit is often enforced. It is a nice respite in an otherwise busy and congested area. The lakes are popular with fishermen. Boats are available for rental.

For Detailed Information
Forest Preserve District of Cook County
536 N. Harlem Ave.
River Forest, IL 60305   708-366-9420

NIPC
400 W. Madison St.
Chicago, IL 60606   312-454-0400

For Calendar of Events
in Surrounding Communities
Elk Grove Village Hall
901 Wellington Ave.
Elk Grove Village, IL 60007   708-439-7302

Schaumburg Municipal Bldg.
101 S. Schaumburg Ct.
Schaumburg, IL 60193   708-894-4500

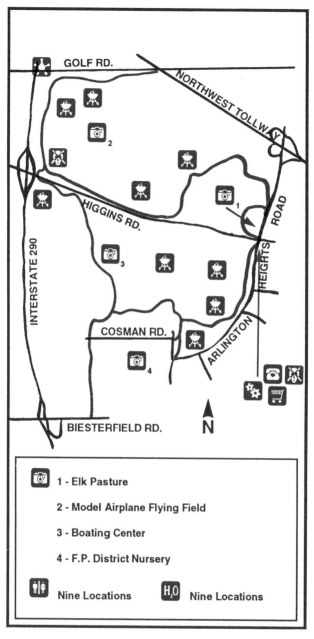

Directions for parking: Rt. 53 to Higgins Rd. (Rt. 72), east .25 miles to entrance on the right or Golf Road .25 miles east of Rt. 53.

Chicago Lakefront Bike Trail

Trail Distance . . . . 20 Miles
Trail Surface . . . . Blacktop
Type of Use . . . . Tour
Towns . . . . Chicago
County . . . . Cook

Author's Comments: By far the most interesting and colorful bike trail in the entire area. Lots of use, especially in the summer on nice weekends. The most used portion is from McCormick Place to Belmont, which includes Miegs Field Airport, the Shedd Aquarium, Adler Planetarium, Field Museum, Grant Park, Buckingham Fountain (one block west), Burnham Harbor, Navy Pier, Oak Street Beach, and Lincoln Park. People-watching galore makes the trip a fascinating experience. At the far south end at 71st Street, don't miss the restored South Shore Country Club (used in the film ''Blues Brothers''). For safety's sake, women, ride this with a companion.

Connecting Trails: There is a designated street route at Ardmore that leads to the Evanston Lakeshore Trail. There is a similar street connection to the North Branch Trail beginning at Bryn Mawr.

For Detailed Information
Cycle Chicago,
Bureau of Traffic Engineering
320 N. Clark St.
Chicago, IL 60610   312-744-4686

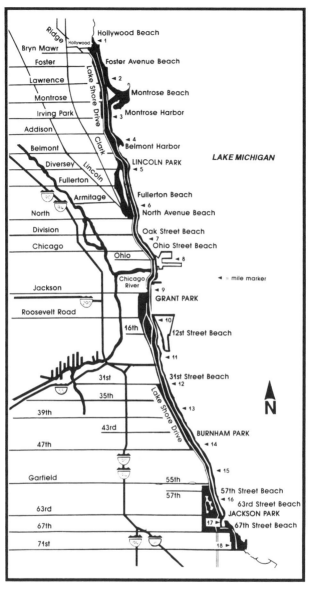

Directions for parking: Lake Shore Drive to any of the cross streets shown above.

Deer Grove Trail

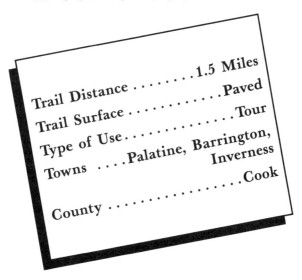

Trail Distance . . . . .1.5 Miles
Trail Surface . . . . .Paved
Type of Use. . . . . .Tour
Towns . . . .Palatine, Barrington, Inverness
County . . . . .Cook

Author's Comments: This is a short, but pleasant trail and is a good place to park if you plan to use the Palatine trail.

Connecting trails: Palatine Bicycle Trail connects at Quentin Road and Dundee Road.

For Detailed Information
Forest Preserve District of Cook County
536 N. Harlem Ave.
River Forest, IL 60305   708-366-9420

For Calendar of Events
in Surrounding Communities
Greater Palatine
Chamber of Commerce and Ind.
Carol Pape, Pres.
17 E. Northwest Hwy.
Palatine, IL 60067   708-359-7200

Barrington Area Chamber of Commerce
Carole Beese, Pres.
325 N. Hough St.
Barrington, IL 60010   708-381-2525

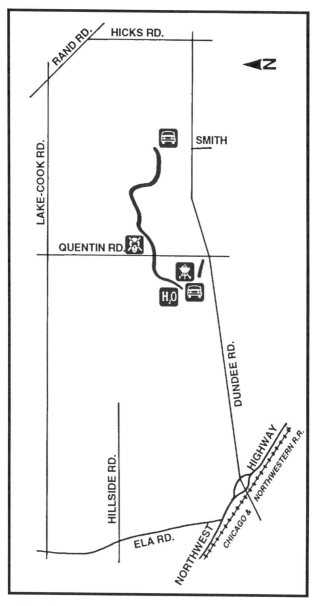

Directions for parking: Rt. 53 to Dundee Rd.
west, 3.8 miles. East parking access is just past
Hicks Rd. on right. Trail starts at far end of the
parking lot.

Evanston-Chicago Connection

Trail Distance . . . . 4.5 Miles
Trail Surface . . . . Streets
Type of Use . . . . Tour
Towns . . . . Evanston, Chicago
County . . . . Cook

Author's Comments: The city, in conjunction with the Chicagoland Bicycle Federation, has done their best to find low-traffic side streets for a safe and efficient trip between two outstanding lakefront trails. For a truly different eating experience stop at the Heartland Cafe on 7000 N. Glenwood Ave. The ambiance is akin to a 60's coffee house and the cuisine is nouveau health food.

Connecting trails: Evanston Lakeshore from the north, Chicago Lake Front from the south.

For Detailed Information
Cycle Chicago
Bureau of Traffic Engineering
320 N. Clark St., Room 402
Chicago, IL 60610   312-744-4686

Chicagoland Bicycle Federation
P.O. Box 64396
Chicago, IL 60664   312-42-PEDAL

For other bikeway information
for the City of Chicago
Cook County Forest Preserve District
312-261-8400

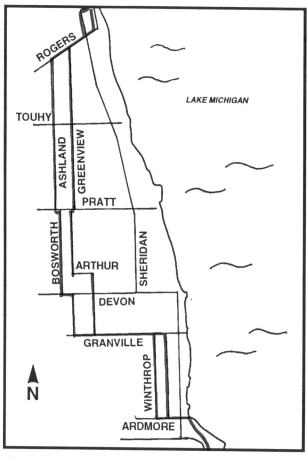

Directions for parking: Lake Shore Drive north to Hollywood.

Chicago Park District   312-294-2200

**Northeastern Illinois Planning Commission
400 West Madison
Chicago, IL 60606   312-454-0400**

*For Calendar of Events
in Surrounding Communities*
**City Clerk, Civic Center
2100 Ridge Ave.
Evanston, IL 60201   708-328-2100**

**Chicago City Hall
121 N. LaSalle Ave.
Chicago, IL 60602   312-744-5000**

Evanston-
Lake Shore Trail

Trail Distance . . . . 7 Miles

Trail Surface . . . . Concrete & blacktop

Type of Use . . . . Tour

Towns . . . . Evanston

County . . . . Cook

Author's Comments: Most of the northern portion of this trail is on sidewalks where pedestrian traffic can be heavy. It is one of the most interesting trails in the area, however, and should not be missed. Don't miss the loop that goes around the lake side of Northwestern Campus. You'll even find a marina operated by the University where you can sign up for sailing lessons. There is a nice beach accompanied by a park just south of the campus.

Other trail connections: The connection from the south to the Chicago Lakefront Bike Trail (4.5 miles) is well marked by ''Bike Route'' signage and follows low-traffic side streets. The connection from the north to the Green Bay Trail in Wilmette (1.5 miles) is not well-marked and is tricky to accomplish.

For Detailed Information
City Clerk, Civic Center
2100 Ridge Ave.
Evanston, IL 60201   708-328-2100

NIPC
400 W. Madison St.
Chicago, IL 60606   312-454-0400

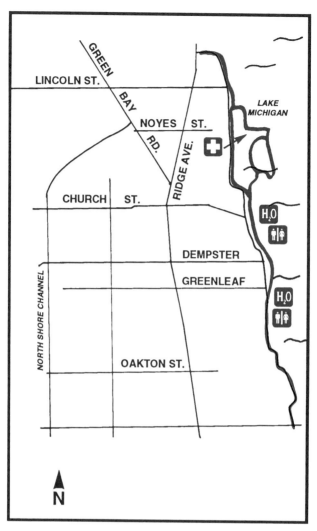

LINCOLN ST.

GREEN BAY RD.

NOYES ST.

RIDGE AVE.

CHURCH ST.

DEMPSTER

GREENLEAF

OAKTON ST.

NORTH SHORE CHANNEL

LAKE MICHIGAN

H₂0

H₂0

N

Directions for parking: Parking is available at various places along Sheridan Rd., especially at the south end. However, this is a busy area and you may have to search for an open spot.

For Calendar of Events
in Surrounding Communities
City of Evanston
c/o City Clerk, Civic Center
2100 Ridge Ave.
Evanston, IL 60201   708-328-2100

Green Bay Trail

Trail Distance	10 Miles
Trail Surface	Paved and crushed limestone
Type of Use	Tour
Towns	Wilmette, Kenilworth, Winnetka, Glencoe, Highland Park
County	Cook

Author's Comments: The Kenilworth portion of this trail allows the biker the opportunity to jump off the trail and cruise the side streets to observe ritzy communities. This trail follows the NW RR and a fence generally protects riders from the tracks. The farther north you ride, the more street crossings you encounter and the less interesting the trail becomes. There are a few tricky places where the trail seems to end, or jumps onto streets. The general rule of thumb is to stay close to the tracks. You'll pick up the trail again.

Connecting trails: Evanston Lakeshore to the south. Lake Forest/Lake Bluff to the north. North Branch to the west.

For Detailed Information
NIPC
400 W. Madison St.
Chicago, IL 60606   312-454-0400
(Lake County portion of Green Bay
Trail only)

For Calendar of Events
in Surrounding Communities
Wilmette Village Hall
1200 Wilmette Ave.
Wilmette, IL 60091   708-251-2700

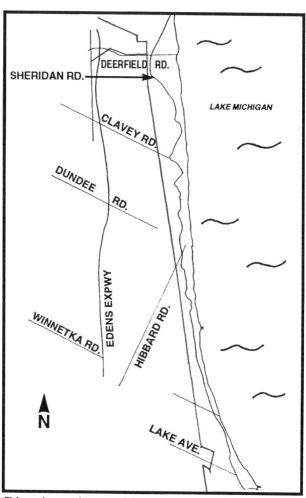

Directions for parking: Parking is generally available along Green Bay Rd. and NW Commuter Stations in Wilmette and Kenilworth. You must cross the tracks to pick up the trail.

Glencoe Village Center
325 Hazel
Glencoe, IL 60022   708-835-4111

Winnetka Chamber of Commerce
Joan L. Moreland, Exec. Dir.
841 Spruce St.
Winnetka, IL 60093   708-446-4451

Highland Park Chamber of Commerce
Virginia Collins, Exec. Dir.
600 Central Ave., #205
Highland Park, IL 60035   708-432-0284

I & M Canal Trail

Trail Distance ·········9 Miles
Trail Surface ·········Blacktop
Type of Use·············Tour
Towns ········Willow Springs
County ···············Cook

Author's Comments: This trail has a 3 mile loop at each end and a 2 mile center section. It is located between the old I & M Canal and the Illinois Sanitary & Ship Canal at the northern end of an extensive area of forest preserves. If you're a mountain biker, be sure to explore the other forest preserves in the area.

Nearby trails: Arie Crown and Tinley Creek

For Detailed Information
Forest Preserve District of Cook County
536 N. Harlem Ave.
River Forest, IL 60305   708-366-9420

For Calendar of Events
in Surrounding Communities
LaGrange West Suburban
Chamber of Commerce
Peter Solie, Executive Director
512 W. Burlington Ave., P.O. Box 187
LaGrange, IL 60525   708-352-0494

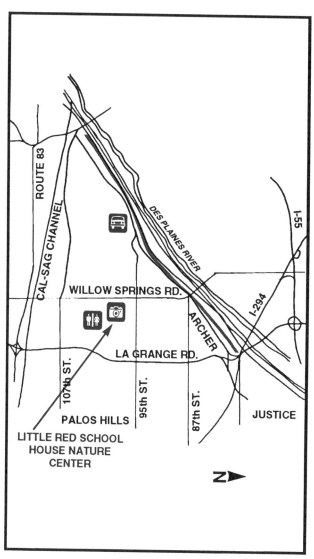

Directions for parking: I-55 exit south on Rt. 45-12-20 to Rt. 171 (Archer Rd.) west. Turn off one block east of Willow Springs Rd. Go a half block north, then west under bridge to parking lot. I-294 has an exit northbound at 79th St. and and exit southbound at I-55.

Illinois Prairie Path (East Section)

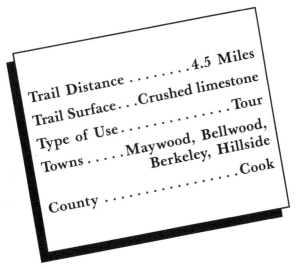

Trail Distance . . . . 4.5 Miles
Trail Surface . . . Crushed limestone
Type of Use . . . . Tour
Towns . . . . . Maywood, Bellwood, Berkeley, Hillside
County . . . . Cook

Author's Comments: This trail begins at 1st Ave. directly west from the 4th District Cook County Building. Fast food is available along 1st Ave. Heading west, the Maywood/Bellwood portions of this trail have been improved. A playground is available on the northeast corner of 17th Ave. From 19th to 25th Ave., the view is unattractive - industrial backyards don't make for "scenic" terrain. When you cross 25th Ave., hop south to Madison Street to avoid the RR underpass, which is not rideable. From Hillside west to Elmhurst, you ride through residential areas. This is a very flat portion of the Prairie Path.

Connecting trails: Illinois Prairie Path continues to the west, Elmhurst is the next town (See DuPage County).

For Detailed Information
The Illinois Prairie Path
P.O. Box 1086 • Wheaton, IL 60189

NIPC • 400 W. Madison St.
Chicago, IL 60606   312-454-0400

For Calendar of Events
in Surrounding Communities
Maywood Village Hall • 115 S. 5th Ave.
Maywood, IL 60153   708-344-1260

Directions for parking: I-290 (Eisenhower Expy.) Exit north on Rt. 45 Mannheim Rd., .5 miles to Rt. 56 (Butterfield), west .5 miles. Trailhead is behind small church on right. Parking also available along Electric Ave. in Hillside and Berkeley.

North Branch Trail

Trail Distance . . . . 20.1 Miles
Trail Surface . . . . Blacktop
Type of Use . . Tour or Mountain
Towns . . . Chicago, Lincolnwood, Skokie, Morton Grove, Glenview, Northfield, Northbrook, Glencoe
County . . . . Cook

Author's Comments: One of the more popular trails in the area. It follows the north branch of the Chicago River and is usually winding through one forest preserve or another. There are a few tricky crossings of major cross streets, but for the most part the trail is quite scenic and enjoyable. The Chicago Botanic Gardens at the north end should not be missed. If you start the trail from the south end and head north and want to dine at the Garden, please do so. There are many other overheated bikers joining you in the cafeteria line. Touhy Ave. intersection is extremely dangerous. The path narrows, grooved ruts between the sidewalk, curb and road topple many bicyclers. We observed two near bike-on-bike collisions at Touhy Ave. Try walking your bike across! It is easy to take the wrong fork between Lake and Winnetka Rd. One dead ends at Winnetka Rd. You can take either side of the loop north of Willow Rd.

Connections: This trail will eventually connect with the Green Bay Bicycle Trail on the north end. You could take Peterson Ave. east to connect with the Lake Front Trail.

Connections: This trail will eventually connect with the Green Bay Bicycle Trail on the north end. You could take Peterson Ave. east to connect with the Lake Front Trail.

Directions for parking:
1. Chicago Botanic Garden (North Trailhead) I-94 Edens Expy. Exit east on Lake-Cook Rd. (County Line Rd.)
2. Parking at all the rest stops/points of interest.
3. Whealan Pool (South Trailhead)

A. I-94 exit west on Peterson Ave./Caldwell intersection. Go west on Devon. Directly east of the Milwaukee Ave. interesection, turn north into Whealan Pool Forest Preserve Entrance and park.

B. I-90, Exit north on Harlem Ave. Turn east on Devon Ave. Directly east of Milwaukee Ave. intersection on the north side of Devon is the Whealan Pool Forest Preserve Entrance.

See map on following page

For Detailed Information
Forest Preserve District of Cook County
536 N. Harlem Ave., River Forest, IL 60305
708-366-9420   312-261-8400

For Calendar of Events
in Surrounding Communities
Chicago City Hall
121 N. LaSalle Ave.
Chicago, IL 60602   312-744-5000

Lincolnwood Chamber of Commerce
Marlene May, President/CEO
4433 W. Touhy Ave., #264
Lincolnwood, IL 60646   708-679-5760

Skokie Village Hall
5127 Oakton
Skokie, IL 60077   708-673-0500

Morton Grove Village Hall
6101 Capulina Ave.
Morton Grove, IL 60053   708-965-4100

Glenview Village Hall
1225 Waukegan Rd.
Glenview, IL 60025   708-724-1700

Northfield Village Hall
361 Happ Rd.
Northfield, IL 60053   708-446-9200

Northbrook Village Hall
1225 Cedar Lane
Northbrook, IL 60062   708-272-5050

Glencoe Village Center
325 Hazel
Glencoe, IL 60022   708-835-4111

 1 - Chicago Botanic Garden

2 - Skokie Lagoons

3 - Blue Star Memorial Woods

4 - Glenview Woods

5 - Harms Woods

6 - Chick Evans Golf Course

7 - Linne Woods

8 - Miami Woods

9 - Clayton Smith Woods

10 - Whealan Pool

11 - Edgebrook Golf Course

12 - Billy Caldwell Golf Course

1 - Cafeteria at Botanic Gardens

2 - Hot Dog Stand

H₂O Available at most parking lots along the trail

and   Along the trail

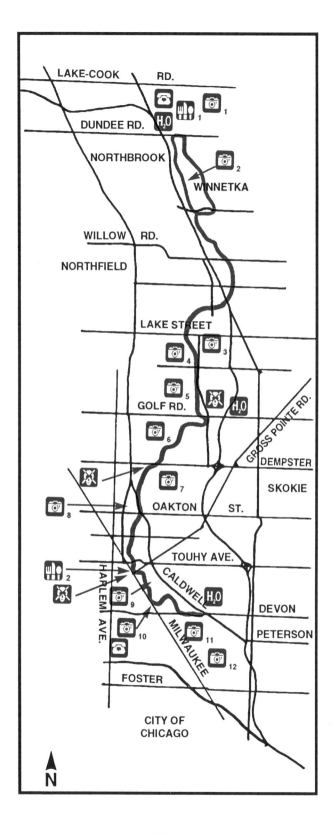

North Shore Channel Trail

Trail Distance	5.0 Miles
Trail Surface	Blacktop
Type of Use	Tour
Towns	Evanston
County	Cook

Author's Comments: This rather short trail follows the North Shore Channel on the western edge of Evanston. The channel is bordered on both sides by parks and pleasant residential surroundings. Some of the street crossings can be tricky. There is a break in the trail between Lake and Church streets where you must follow the streets around an elementary school. It is easy to get lost here. Given the short length of the trail, it is probably best enjoyed by local residents or those cycling from the Evanston Lake Shore Trail on the east to the North Branch Trail 3.5 miles further west.

Connecting trails: Evanston Lake Shore Trail to the east ½ mile. North Branch Trail to the west 3¾ mile. Green Bay Trail to the north 1¼ mile.

For Detailed Information
NIPC
400 W. Madison St.
Chicago, IL 60606   312-454-0400

City Clerk, Civic Center
2100 Ridge Ave.
Evanston, IL 60201   708-328-2100

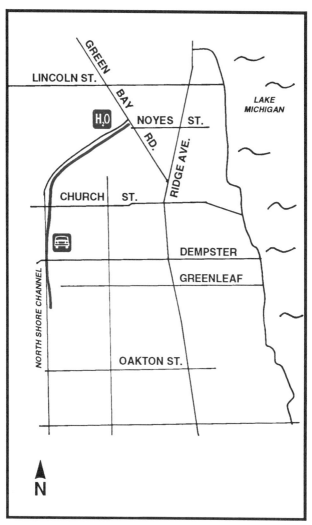

Directions for parking: Oakton to McCormick, north .5 mile to Main St., east across the channel to McDaniel north. Park along the street adjacent to the park and trail.

*For Calendar of Events
in Surrounding Communities*
**City Clerk, Civic Center
2100 Ridge Ave.
Evanston, IL 60201   708-328-2100**

Palatine Trail

Trail Distance . . . . 4.5 Miles
Trail Surface . . . . Paved
Type of Use . . . . Tour
Towns . . . . Palatine
County . . . . Cook

Author's Comments: This trail challenges you with interesting and changing terrain including changing grades. Nice path, good length.

Connecting trails: Deer Grove Bike Trail

For Detailed Information
Palatine Park District
250 East Wood St.
Palatine, IL 60067   708-991-0333

For Calendar of Events
in Surrounding Communities
Greater Palatine
Chamber of Commerce and Ind.
17 E. Northwest Hwy.
Palatine, IL 60067   708-359-7200

Directions for parking: I suggest you park at Deer Grove Bike Trail. Take I-294 to Rt. 68 west (Dundee Rd.). Cross Rt. 53. Turn north on Quentin Rd. then west at Deer Grove Parking Access. For Trailhead parking, take I-294 to Palatine Rd. west. Cross Rt. 53, turn north on Winston Dr., go 7-8 blocks and turn west on Anderson Dr. Park alongside the playground.

Thorn Creek Trail

Trail Distance . . . . 7.8 Miles
Trail Surface . . . . Paved
Type of Use . . . . Tour
Towns . . . . Park Forest,
South Chicago Heights,
Lansing, Glenwood
County . . . . Cook

Author's Comments: Lansing Woods trail skirts Torrence Ave. for a noisy ride due to traffic. After crossing Torrence and entering North Creek Meadow, the noise diminishes. I saw a huge hawk in this Meadow, and a bluebird (not a bluejay). The Sauk Trail Lake Trail is heavily wooded. The trail follows the perimeter of the Lake. I saw four deer, among them twin fawns. The deer are so adept at camouflage that they stand alongside the trail as you whiz by on your bike. Slow down and try to view them drinking at the Lake. Nice trail.

Connecting trails: Plans are underway (as indicated by the dots on the map) for extending the trails alongside Thorn Creek to connect Lansing Woods to Sauk Trail Lake. Take Western Ave. South to connect with the University Park South Bikeway System (Park Forest South).

For Detailed Information
Forest Preserve District of Cook County
536 N. Harlem Ave., River Forest, IL 60305
312-261-8400   708-366-9420

Directions for parking:
North Trail (Lansing Woods): Take I-294, exit 394 (Calumet Expy.) south. Take 186th east past Torrence Ave. Entrance on south side of 186th St.
South Trail & (Sauk Trail Lake): Take I-294, exit Rt. 1 (Halsted Ave.) south. Take Rt. 30 (Lincoln Hwy.) west, Ashland south, 26th St. west. Entrance on south side of 26th St.

For Calendar of Events
in Surrounding Communities
South Chicago Heights Village Hall
2729 Jackson Ave.
South Chicago Heights, IL 60411
708-755-1880

Chamber of Commerce of the Parks
Doris Finout, Exec. Dir.
13 Centre, P.O. Box 1949
Park Forest, IL 60466   708-481-5390

Lansing Mayor and Clerks Office
18200 Chicago Ave.
Lansing, IL 60438   708-895-7200

Tinley Creek Trail

Trail Distance . . . . 8.8 Miles
Trail Surface . . . . Blacktop
Type of Use . . . . Tour
Towns . . . . Orland Park,
Tinley Park, Country Club Hills,
Oak Forest
County . . . . Cook

Author's Comments: The first 1.5 miles on the east side of Central Ave. is adjacent to the highway. This trail is extremely noisy from traffic and not particularly scenic. The mid-section of the trail is through wooded areas, while the northern portion is mixed woods, prairie and residential.

For Detailed Information
Forest Preserve District of Cook County
536 N. Harlem Ave., River Forest, IL 60305
312-261-9400   708-366-9420

For Calendar of Events
in Surrounding Communities
Oak Forest City Hall
15440 Central Ave.
Oak Forest, IL 60452   708-687-4050

Orland Park Village Hall
14415 Beacon Ave.
Orland Park, IL 60462   708-349-5400

Tinley Park Village Hall
17355 68th Ct.
Tinley Park, IL 60477   708-532-7700

Country Club Hills City Hall
3700 W. 175th Pl.
Country Club Hills, IL 60477
708-798-2616

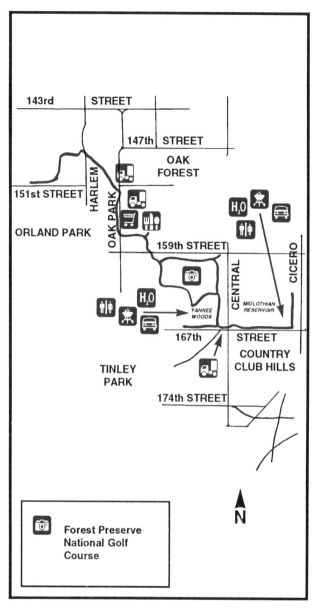

Directions for parking: Take 167th St. west of Cicero at Midlothian Reservoir and on the west side of Central Ave., go north of 167th Street at Yankee Woods.

Kane County Trails

Fox River-Mid
Fox River-North
Fox River-South
Great Western
Illinois Prairie Path
Virgil Gilman

Fox River Trail (Mid)
(Elgin to Geneva)

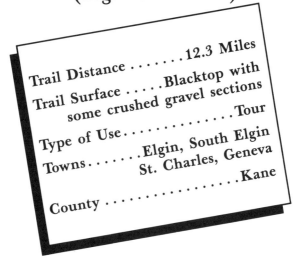

Trail Distance . . . . 12.3 Miles

Trail Surface . . . . . Blacktop with some crushed gravel sections

Type of Use . . . . Tour

Towns . . . . Elgin, South Elgin St. Charles, Geneva

County . . . . Kane

Author's Comments: From the Prairie Path Junction, go south under the rail bridge and across the creek. At this point, there is a stretch which is like a roller coaster with short ups-and-downs winding through some woods. Lots of fun, but be careful! The trail from the Trolley Museum to St. Charles is particularly beautiful. It is also scenic and well traveled from St. Charles to Fabyan Park. This is truly one of Illinois' premier trails. The points of interest, the variety of scenery, the ease of use, and the abundance of facilities and places to eat make this a trail not to be missed.

Connecting trails: The Illinois Prairie Path North Branch joins the trail just south of Elgin. The trail continues north 15 miles to Crystal Lake and south 8.3 miles to Aurora. The Great Western Trail begins west of St. Charles. The Fox River Trail continues on the east side of the Fox River and crosses the river in Batavia where the Trail is named ''Fox River West'' and continues to the Virgil L. Gilman trail in Aurora.

Technical Comments: If you start somewhere other than Hopp Rd. in South Elgin, be sure to cross the River on the Hopp Road Bridge or you will lose the trail. From Valley View to

Delnor Hospital, you will find that the trail alternates to occasional street riding. Follow the Bike Route signs between Delnor Hospital and Illinois St. in St. Charles where the trail stops temporarily. The trail also leaves the river and jogs across Rt. 25 between Rt. 64 and Rt. 38.

Directions for parking:
North End: I-90 west or Rt. 20 to Rt. 25, south to Bartlett Rd., west to River (Bartlett becomes Hopp Rd.)
South End: I-88 to Farnsworth, north 1 mile to Rt. 56, west 2.2 miles to Rt. 25, north 4 miles to Fabian Park.

See map on page 54

For Detailed Information
Fox Valley Living
Sampler Publications, Inc.
707 Kautz Rd.
St. Charles, IL 60174   708-377-7570

NIPC • 400 West State St.
Chicago, IL 60606   312-454-0400

Mill Race Cyclery
FOX RIVER TRAIL GUIDE
11 E. State (Rt. 38)
Geneva, IL 60134   708-232-2833

For Calendar of Events
in Surrounding Communities
Elgin Area Convention & Visitors Bureau
24 E. Chicago St.
Elgin, IL 60120   708-695-7540

Elgin Chamber of Commerce
708-741-5660

Greater St. Charles
Convention & Visitors Bureau
Dept. K, P.O. Box 11, 201 First Ave.
St. Charles, IL 60174   708-377-6161

Geneva Chamber of Commerce
Dept. K, 5 North Third St.
Geneva, IL 60134   708-232-6060

Fox River Trail
(North Segment of Fox River Trail Algonquin to Elgin)

Trail Distance . . . . 11.7 Miles

Trail Surface . . . . . Blacktop with some crushed gravel sections

Type of Use . . . . Tour

Towns . . . . Algonquin, Carpentersville, W. Dundee, E. Dundee, Elgin

County . . . . Kane

Author's Comments: One reward for riding this trail is Trails & Treasures in Elgin. It has a quiet, riverside view and offers homemade sandwiches and sweets for ragged bicyclers. Another reward is the homemade ice cream at the shop 1 block west of the E. Dundee Train Station. The trail ends abruptly in downtown Elgin. Unmarked and confusing as it is, the rule of thumb is to take streets as close to the river as possible.

Connecting trails: Prairie Trail South in McHenry County. Directly north, this trail connects in Algonquin from Crystal Lake. Voyageurs Landing Forest Preserve or the Fox River Trail offer a turn west under I-90, crosses the river and forks on the other side. If you turn right (north), you will go to Voyageurs Landing Forest Preserve. If you turn left (south), you will go to Tyler Creek Forest Preserve. The trail to Tyler Creek is a few miles. Try both.

The Illinois Prairie Path intersects at the southern segment of this trail in South Elgin of DuPage County.

See map on page 54

See map on page 54

For Detailed Information
Fox Valley Living
Sampler Publications, Inc.
707 Kautz Rd.
St. Charles, IL 60174   708-377-7570

Directions for parking:
Algonquin: I-90 west to Rt. 31, north to Rt. 62, west for about a mile. Park alongside the road east of Pyott Rd.
Elgin: I-90 to 25 south, to Chicago St. Park in public lots. (Park at the Intersection of the Illinois Prairie Path a few miles south of Rt. 20 on Raymond St.)

For Calendar of Events
in Surrounding Communities
Algonquin Village Hall
2 S. Main St.
Algonquin, IL 60102   815-658-3244

Elgin Area Convention & Visitors Bureau
24 E. Chicago St.
Elgin, IL 60120   708-695-7540

Elgin Chamber of Commerce
708-741-5660

Fox River Trail
(South Segment of Fox River Trail Batavia to Aurora)

Trail Distance . . . . 8.4 Miles

Trail Surface . . . . Paved and crushed limestone

Type of Use . . . . Tour

Towns . . . . Batavia, North Aurora, Aurora

County . . . . Kane

Author's Comments: The north portion of this trail is tricky to follow through Batavia. On the west side of the river you pass the treatment plant and follow the street. Cross at the light and pick up the trail at the Depot. On the east side (Red Oak Trail) follow the street for one block on each side of Fabyan Parkway.

Connecting trails: Fox River Trail (East) connects to the north. Virgil Gilman Trail - Bike south on Rt. 31 approximately 2 miles to pick up this trail west to Bliss Woods Forest Preserve or east thru Aurora. Cross the bridge at Fabyan Forest Preserve and bike south along the east side of River to Red Oak Trail. The west side of this river trail is called the Fox River Trail West. The east side is called the Red Oak Trail and is considered part of the Illinois Prairie Path. Midway between Batavia and North Aurora on the Red Oak Trail, the Illinois Prairie Path connects going southwest. We have titled that portion of the I.P.P. the SW Branch. It is located in DuPage County.

See map on following page

For Detailed Information
Fox Valley Living/
Sampler Publications, Inc.
707 Kautz Rd.
St. Charles, IL 60174   708-377-7570

Directions for parking: I-88 to Farnsworth, south 2.5 miles to New York Ave. west 2 miles. There is a parking lot just across the river on the right. Trail begins at the north end of the lot.

For Calendar of Events
in Surrounding Communities
Batavia Chamber of Commerce
Dept. K, 327 W. Wilson
Batavia, IL 60510   708-879-7134

Greater Aurora Chamber of Commerce
Dept. K, 40 W. Downer Pl.
P.O. Box 72
Aurora, IL 60507   708-897-9214

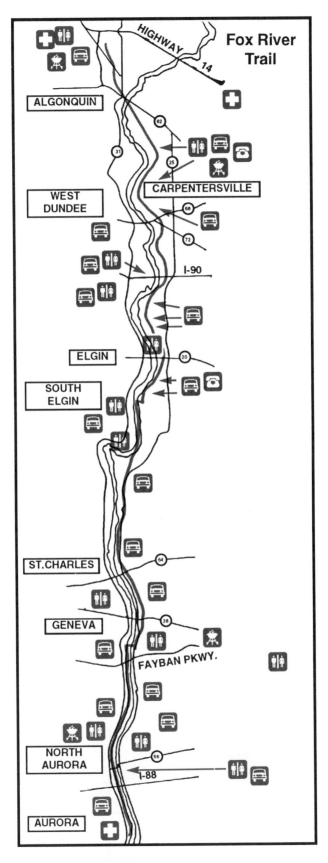

Great Western Trail

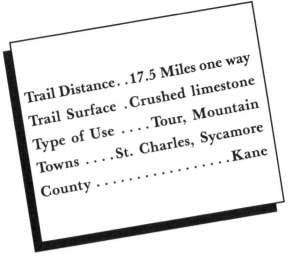

Trail Distance..17.5 Miles one way
Trail Surface .Crushed limestone
Type of Use ....Tour, Mountain
Towns ....St. Charles, Sycamore
County ....Kane

Author's Comments: This trail follows the abandoned Great Western Railroad line. Most of the trail runs alongside Rt. 64. There is one section through a forest preserve. For the most part, the trail offers views of suburban housing developments or farm fields. Not the most interesting trail, but nice for distance and sparsity of crossings. Sycamore has an ice cream stand less than a mile west of the trail end and a very nice park still closer to the trail. The park has golf, swimming, rest rooms and a snack shop. The forested area west of Wasco has some nice off-road trails for trail bikes. Mile markers start at the Kane/De Kalb county line (13.5 miles from trailhead). This is a popular ride the weekend before Halloween when Sycamore celebrates their annual Pumpkinfest.

For Detailed Information
Kane County Forest Preserve District
719 Batavia Ave.
Geneva, IL 60134   708-232-5981

Fox Valley Living/
Sampler Publications, Inc.
707 Kautz Rd.
St. Charles, IL 60174   708-377-7570

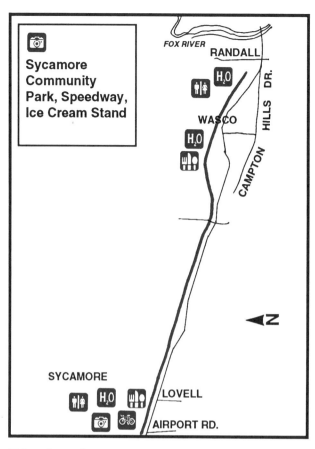

Sycamore Community Park, Speedway, Ice Cream Stand

FOX RIVER
RANDALL
WASCO
CAMPTON HILLS DR.
N
SYCAMORE
LOVELL
AIRPORT RD.

Directions for parking:
St. Charles: Rt. 64 to Randall Rd. north .5 miles to Dean St. west .5 miles to park on south side of road.
Sycamore: Trail ends .3 miles east of Sycamore Community Park ½ block north of Rt. 64.

*For Calendar of Events
in Surrounding Communities*
Greater St. Charles
Convention & Visitors Bureau
Dept. K, P.O. Box 11, 201 First Ave.
St. Charles, IL 60174   708-377-6161

Greater Sycamore Chamber of Commerce
Ms. Larry Kaye Gray, Exec. Mgr.
206 W. State St.
Sycamore, IL 60178   815-895-3456

Illinois Prairie Path-
Batavia Spur

Trail Distance · · · · · · · ·6.5 Miles
Trail Surface · Crushed limestone
Type of Use· · · · · · · · · · · · ·Tour
Towns · · · · ·Batavia, Warrenville
County · · · · · · · · · · · · · · ·Kane

Author's Comments: This is part of the Illinois Prairie Path. When traveling west from Warrenville, the trail forks after about a mile. The more northerly fork follows the old spur line of the CA&E RR to the Fox River and is a bit more scenic than the southerly fork to Aurora. Just before reaching the river, there is another paved trail leading off to the south. It will lead through some woods to the Red Oak Nature Center — which is well worth a stop any time of year. If you continue on the Red Oak Loop, you will end up at the River and cross a bridge to meet the Fox River Trail. Or you can get on the East side of the Fox River Trail by skipping the Red Oak Loop and continuing on the spur. A lot of people make a 50 mile triangle using the Fox River Trail, the northwest, and southwest branches of the Prairie Path.

Connecting trails: Illinois Prairie Path SW Spur on east and Red Oak Trail on west.

For Detailed Information
The Illinois Prairie Path
P.O. Box 1086 • Wheaton, IL 60189

For Calendar of Events in Surrounding Communities
Batavia Chamber of Commerce
Dept. K, 326 W. Wilson
Batavia, IL 60510   708-879-7134

Warrenville City Hall
28 W. 630 Stafford Pl.
Warrenville, IL 60555   708-393-9427

For Info on Red Oak Nature Center & Red Oak Trail
Fox Valley Park District
P.O. Box 818, 712 S. River
Aurora, IL 60507   708-897-0516

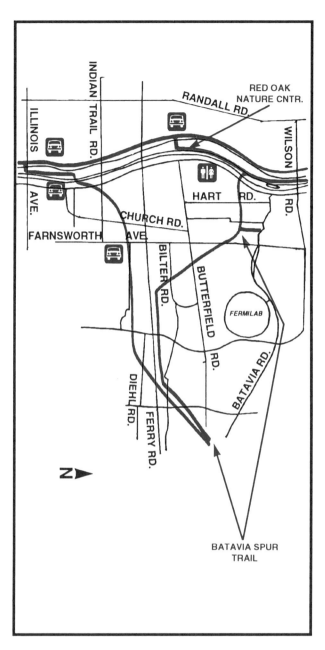

Vehicle parking: Park at Col. Fabyan Forest Preserve (See Fox River Trail) or along Prairie Path at Batavia Rd. & Rt. 56 in Warrenville.

Virgil L. Gilman Nature Trail

Trail Distance...10 Miles one way

Trail Surface ....Crushed gravel and paved

Type of Use...............Tour

Towns.....Montgomery, Aurora

County................Kane

Author's Comments: I recommend beginning the trail at Jericho Rd. just west of the Fox River. Eastbound from Jericho has numerous street crossings, is not well marked, and is not at all scenic. The west portion is through several lovely wooded areas and ends at Bliss Woods which offers camping and hiking.

Connecting trails:
North: The Fox River Trail & the Red Oak Trail.
NE: Illinois Prairie Path Eastbound.
NW: The Great Western Trail.

For Detailed Information
The Fox Valley Park District
P.O. Box 818
Aurora, IL 60507   708-897-0516

For Calendar of Events
in Surrounding Communities
Greater Aurora Chamber of Commerce
Dept. K, 40 W. Downer Pl.
P.O. Box 72
Aurora, IL 60507   708-897-9214

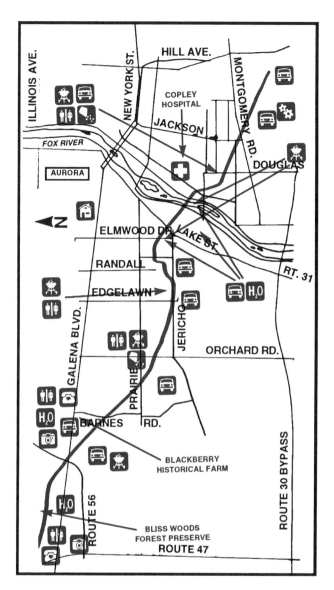

Directions for parking:
Aurora: From I-88 go south 3.8 miles on Farnsworth to Fifth, west .3 miles to Hill, south 2.8 miles to trailhead (just past Montgomery). For Jericho Rd. (Aurora) parking, take Farnsworth south 3 miles to New York, west 2 miles across river to Rt. 31, south 1.5 miles to Jericho, west 1 block to parking on the right at Terry Ave.

Lake County Trails

Daniel Wright Woods
Des Plaines River
Grant Woods
Green Belt
Lake Forest/Lake Bluff
Lakewood
McDonald Woods
North Shore Trail
Old School Woods
Vernon Hills
Zion

Daniel Wright Woods Trail

Trail Distance . . . . 5.4 Miles

Trail Surface . . . .
Limestone & packed dirt

Type of Use . . . . Tour, Mountain

Towns . . . . Vernon Hills,
Half Day, Lake Forest

County . . . . Lake

Author's Comments: This is a beautiful trail! It is heavily wooded and runs alongside the Des Plaines river. It's popularity with horsemen makes for an occasional choppy trail. I value it because it is quiet, serene and away from any traffic noise.

Nearby trails: Grant Woods to the southwest and Des Plaines River Trail to the northeast.

For Detailed Information
Lake County Forest Preserve
2000 N. Milwaukee Ave.
Libertyville, IL 60048   708-367-6640

For Calendar of Events
in Surrounding Communities
Lake Forest City Hall
220 E. Deerpath
Lake Forest, IL 60045   708-234-2600

Lake Forest Chamber of Commerce
Sarah A. Danielson, Exec. Dir.
272 Market Square #10
Lake Forest, IL 60045   708-234-4282

Vernon Hills Village Hall
290 Evergreen Dr.
Vernon Hills, IL 60061   708-367-3700

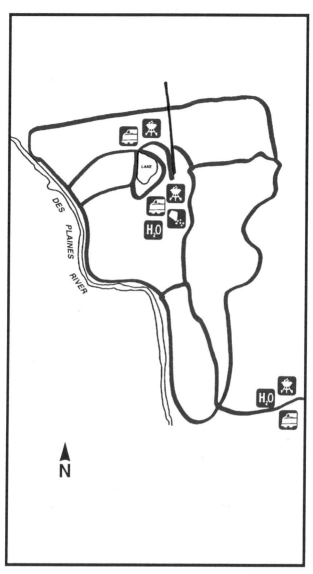

Directions for parking: I-94 to I-60, west to St. Mary's Rd. Turn south to the end. (Road goes east but go straight into forest preserve.)

Des Plaines River Trail

Trail Distance . . . . .8.7 Miles

Trail Surface .Crushed limestone

Type of Use . . . . Tour, Mountain

Towns . . . .
Rosecrans, Wadsworth,
Zion, Winthrop Harbor,
Old Mill Creek, Beach Park

County . . . . .Lake

Author's Comments: One of the prettiest trails in the entire Chicagoland area. A nice blend of woods, prairie and river. Lake County plans on eventually linking with the other trails to follow the Des Plaines River from the Wisconsin border to Cook County. Van Patten Woods offers amenities for a family to spend the entire day picnicking.

Nearby trails: Zion to the east. McDonald Woods to the southwest.

For Detailed Information
Lake County Forest Preserve District
2000 N. Milwaukee Ave.
Libertyville, IL 60048   708-367-6640

For Calendar of Events
in Surrounding Communities
Lake County IL.
Convention & Visitors Bureau
414 N. Sheridan Rd.
Waukegan, IL 60085-4096

Winthrop Harbor City Hall
830 Sheridan Rd.
Winthrop Harbor, IL 60093   708-872-8346

Zion City Hall
2828 Sheridan Rd.
Zion, IL 60099   708-872-4546

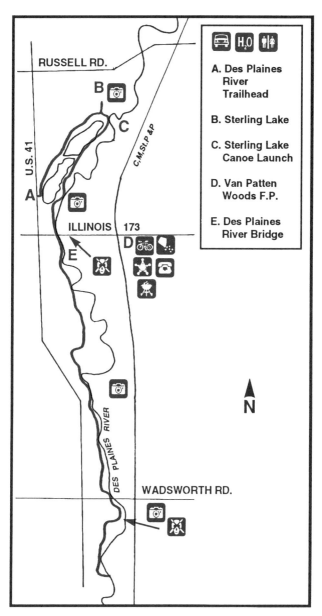

A. Des Plaines River Trailhead

B. Sterling Lake

C. Sterling Lake Canoe Launch

D. Van Patten Woods F.P.

E. Des Plaines River Bridge

RUSSELL RD.

U.S. 41

C.M.St.P.&P.

ILLINOIS 173

DES PLAINES RIVER

WADSWORTH RD.

N

Directions for parking: Take the Tri-State (I-94) to Rt. 173 east. Cross Rt. 41, one block to the entrance on the north side of the road at Van Patten Woods. Parking also at Points A, B, C and E.

Grant Woods Forest Preserve Trail

Trail Distance ...4.5 Miles total
East loop -
3.25 miles crushed gravel -
West loop -
1.25 miles wood chip -

Trail Surface....Crushed gravel,
dirt, mowed grass

Type of Use ....Tour, Mountain

Towns ..Fox Lake, Round Lake,
Volo, Lake Villa

County ....Lake

Author's Comments: East loop has a spectacular view at the top of the hill. Beware of loose gravel areas. West loop was a dirt road and mowed grass. This author got lost. I picked up the wood chip trail at the Rollins Rd. entrance and the trail dead-ended at the Forest Preserve boundary. Try the West loop (if you can find it) at the northernmost part, where it begins and write and tell me if it dead-ends, too.

For Detailed Information
Lake County Forest Preserve District
2000 N. Milwaukee Ave.
Libertyville, IL 60048   708-367-6640

For Calendar of Events
in Surrounding Communities
Fox Lake Village Hall
305 Rt. 59
Fox Lake, IL 60020   708-587-2151

Round Lake Village Hall
322 W. Railroad Ave.
Round Lake, IL 60073   708-546-5400

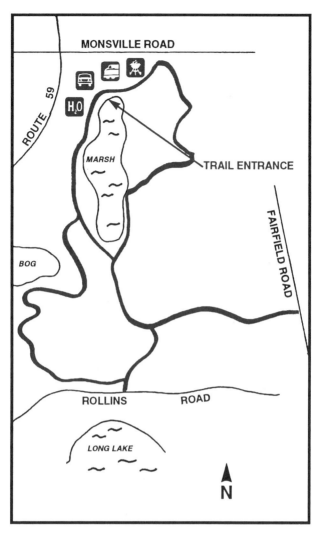

Directions for parking: Tri-State to Rt. 132 west, 10 miles to Rt. 59, south 1.8 miles. Turn east to parking lot.

Lake Villa Village Hall
65 Cedar Ave.
Lake Villa, IL 60046   708-438-5141

Green Belt Forest Preserve Trail

Trail Distance ... 4.2 Miles total
2 miles West loop
2.2 miles East loop

Trail Surface .... Crushed gravel

Type of Use .... Tour, Mountain

Towns .... North Chicago, Waukegan, Gurnee

County .... Lake

Author's Comments: If you're into Prairies, the West Loop is your trail. We did not ride the East loop. Let us know what we missed. Great trail for fledgling bicyclers to learn how to ride.

Nearby trails: Old School to the southwest.

For Detailed Information
Lake County Forest Preserve
2000 N. Milwaukee Ave.
Libertyville, IL 60048   708-367-6640

For Calendar of Events
in Surrounding Communities
North Chicago City Hall
1850 S. Lewis Ave.
North Chicago, IL 60064   708-578-7750

Waukegan Municipal Bldg.
106 N. Utica St.
Waukegan, IL 60079-0888   708-360-9000

Gurnee Village Hall
4573 Grand Ave.
Gurnee, IL 60031   708-673-7650

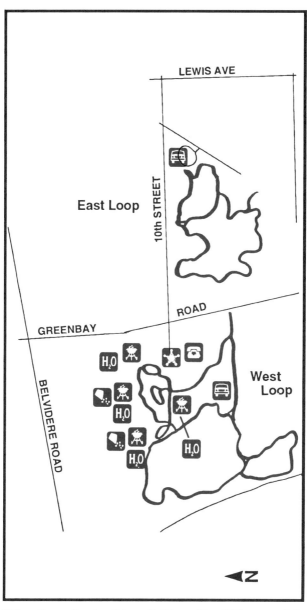

Directions for parking: I-94 to Rt. 120, east 1.6 miles to Rt. 131.

West Loop: South on Rt. 131, West on 10th Street. Park at Shelters. This entrance is open Dec. - April only.

West Loop: South on Rt. 131. Park at trailhead. Entrance open May - Nov. only.

East Loop: South on Rt. 131, east on 10th Street, southwest on Dugdale Rd., West Entrance open year round. Park at Trailhead.

Lake Forest/ Lake Bluff Trail

Trail Distance . . . . 7.5 Miles
Trail Surface . . . . Paved
Type of Use . . . . Tour
Towns . . Lake Bluff, Lake Forest
County . . . . Lake

Author's Comments: Great for family biking. Only three street crossings besides downtown Lake Forest. Between Deerpath & Woodland crossings, you must take the sidewalk on the east side of McKinley Rd. Pavement is rough from Barat College south to Old Elm Rd. (Rt. 52). I suggest you don't roller blade that portion.

Connecting trails: Southern portion at Old Elm Rd. connects with Highland Park Bicycle Path. The northern portion can connect with the North Shore Trail. (See North Shore Trail.)

For Detailed Information
The City of Lake Forest
110 E. Laurel
Lake Forest, IL 60045

Northeastern Illinois Planning Commission
400 W. Madison St.
Chicago, IL 60606   312-454-0400

For Calendar of Events
in Surrounding Communities
Village of Lake Bluff
110 E. Laurel
Lake Bluff, IL 60045   708-234-4150

City of Lake Forest at above address

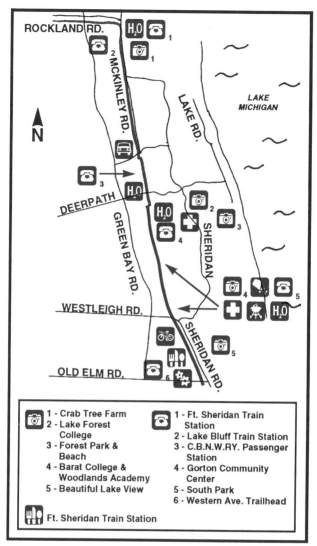

ROCKLAND RD.

MCKINLEY RD.

LAKE RD.

LAKE MICHIGAN

N

DEERPATH

GREEN BAY RD.

SHERIDAN

WESTLEIGH RD.

SHERIDAN RD.

OLD ELM RD.

1 - Crab Tree Farm
2 - Lake Forest College
3 - Forest Park & Beach
4 - Barat College & Woodlands Academy
5 - Beautiful Lake View

1 - Ft. Sheridan Train Station
2 - Lake Bluff Train Station
3 - C.B.N.W.RY. Passenger Station
4 - Gorton Community Center
5 - South Park
6 - Western Ave. Trailhead

Ft. Sheridan Train Station

Directions for parking:
Lake Bluff Trailhead (North): Tri-State to Rockland Rd. (Rt. 176) east. Cross Rt. 43, 41, and 131 (Green Bay Rd.). North on Sheridan then west on 22nd Street and park.
Lake Forest Trailhead (South): Tri-State to Rt. 52 (County A-40) (Old Elm Rd.) east. Cross Rt. 43, 41, and 141. Turn north on Western Ave. directly west of Sheridan Rd. and park.

**Lake Forest Chamber of Commerce
Sarah A. Danielson, Exec. Dir.
272 Market Square #10
Lake Forest, IL 60045   708-234-4282**

Lakewood
Forest Preserve

Trail Distance . . . . 6 Miles
Trail Surface . . . . . . Packed Dirt
(Horse trail)
. . . . Wauconda
Towns . . . . Lake
County . . . .

Author's Comments: This is a strikingly beautiful preserve in a very rural setting. The trail is heavily used by horses - making for very rough riding by even mountain bikes. It should, however, be a real treat for skiers. A trail system for mountain bikes is in the making on the north side of Ivanhoe Road.

Nearby trails: Grant Woods to the north. Wright Woods and Old School to the east.

For Detailed Information
Lake County Forest Preserve District
2000 N. Milwaukee Ave.
Libertyville, IL 60048   708-367-6640

For Calendar of Events
in Surrounding Communities
Wauconda Village Hall
101 N. Main St.
Wauconda, IL 60079-0888   708-526-8786

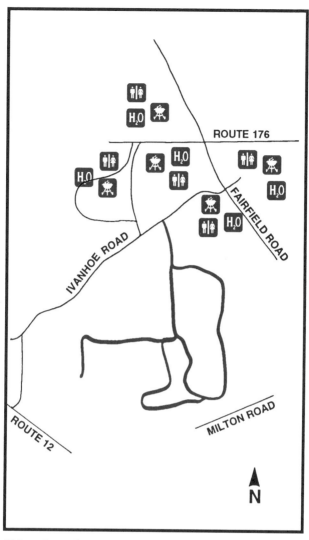

Directions for parking: Tri-State to 176 west 10 miles, Fairfield Road south 1 mile, Ivanhoe Road southwest 1 mile to entrance.

McDonald Forest Preserve Trail

Trail Distance · · · · · · · · · 3 Miles
Trail Surface · · · · · · · · · · · · · · ·
    Crushed gravel/East Loop
    Wood chip/West Loop
Type of Use · · · · Tour, Mountain
Towns · · · Millburn, Lindenhurst
County · · · · · · · · · · · · · · · · Lake

Author's Comments: The wood chip trail is fantastic! This trail might be intended for walking only, so you need to portage your bike around ravines and a creek. Although this trail confuses you with many subsidiary criss-crossing trails, plan on having fun getting lost! Varied ecosystems (woods, ponds, evergreens, dead-woods, prairie, ravines and a creek) combine to make this one of the most beautiful, awe-inspiring and interesting trails to be seen in Chicagoland. Both trails are moderately hilly. The East loop offers vistas to last a lifetime. Be careful of loose gravel on the Eastern loop!

Nearby trails: Des Plaines River Trail to the northeast. Grant Woods to the southwest.

For Detailed Information
Lake County Forest Preserve
2000 N. Milwaukee Ave.
Libertyville, IL 60048   708-367-6640

For Calendar of Events
in Surrounding Communities
Lindenhurst Village Hall
2301 Sand Lake Rd.
Lindenhurst, IL 60046   708-356-8252

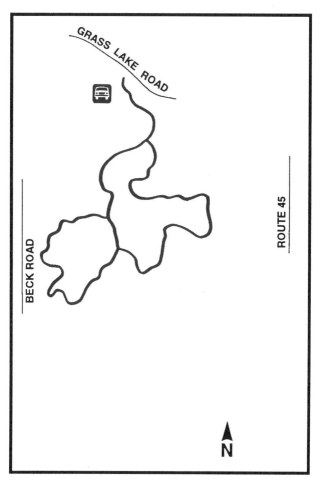

Directions for parking: From the Tri-State Toll-road (I-94) go West on I-132 to Rt. 45, north 3 miles to Grass Lake Road, west 1.3 miles to the south entrance.

North Shore Trail

Trail Distance . . . .
12 Miles to Wisconsin line
15.5 Miles to Kenosha

Trail Surface . . . . Blacktop &
crushed limestone

Type of Use . . . . Tour, Mountain

Towns . . . . North Chicago,
Waukegan, IL Beach State Park,
Zion, Shiloh, Beulah Park,
Winthrop Harbor, Kenosha

County . . . . Lake

Author's Comments: This is a straight line path following the abandoned North Shore Rail line. The southern portion (North Chicago and Waukegan) has numerous cross streets and goes through mixed residential and commercial neighborhoods. This portion is uninteresting. I recommend starting north of Waukegan (the northernmost portion in Illinois). The portion from Zion north becomes less densely populated and more rural, is surrounded by woods on either side and has fewer street crossings. The Wisconsin portion is very pastoral.

Other Trails: This trail continues north to Racine. The Green Bay trail picks up one mile south on Sheridan Rd. across from Great Lakes. Lake Forest/Lake Bluff directly south. Greenbelt Forest Preserve to the west, Old School to the southwest. Des Plaines, River Trail northwest.

For Detailed Information
Lake County Division of Transportation
600 West Winchester Rd.
Libertyville, IL 60048   708-364-3950

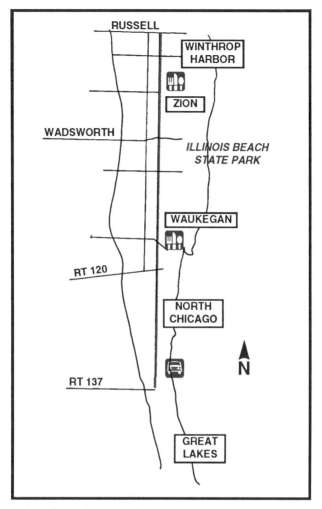

Directions for parking:
North Chicago trailhead: I-94 to Rt. 137 Buckley Rd. east to Lewis Ave., north on 20th Ave., east to Glenn Dr. The trail can be accessed where it crosses any major east-west road from North Chicago to Wisconsin line.

For Calendar of Events
in Surrounding Communities
Lake County Convention
& Visitors Bureau
414 N. Sheridan Rd.
Waukegan, IL 60085-4096

Old School Woods Forest Preserve

Trail Distance . . . . .5.4 Miles

Trail Surface . . . .
Road is paved -
Fitness Trail is wood chips
Bike/Horse Trail is
crushed limestone/dirt

Type of Use . . . . Tour, Mountain

Towns . . . . .Libertyville

County . . . . .Lake

Author's Comments: A great way to spend a day in nature. Pack a lunch, plop down at one of the five shelters (groves), and bike easily on the Roadside within the Preserve. Or choose the more extensive Bicycle/Horse Trail. This Trail provides a pleasant blend of Woods and Prairie. The western portion of this Trail is open terrain and .9 miles, one way. Walk your bikes west on Rockland Road to see the Des Plaines River. You must return via the same route, making this portion approximately 2 miles. This portion has a hill, so take that into account if you are porting children.

Connecting Trails: If you are still up for more trail riding, head south down to St. Mary's Road a few miles to Daniel Wright Woods. Lake County was developing a connecting trail between Old School and Daniel Wright Woods, expected completion Fall of 1992. Greenbelt Forest Preserve to the north.

For Detailed Information
Lake County Forest Preserve District
2000 N. Milwaukee Ave.
Libertyville, IL 60048   708-367-6640

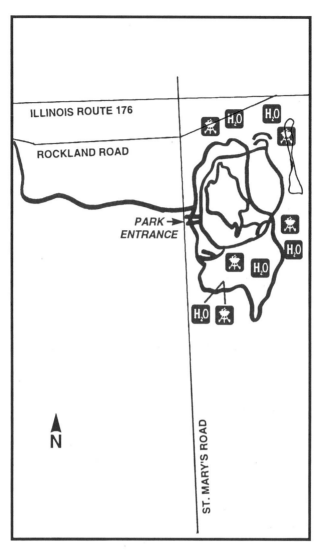

Directions to Trailhead: I-94 to 176 west to St. Mary's Road south. Turn east to Entrance.

*For Calendar of Events
in Surrounding Communities*
Village of Libertyville
200 East Cook
Libertyville, IL 60048   708-362-2430

Vernon Hills Trail

Trail Distance . . . . 1.25 Miles
Trail Surface . . . . Paved
Type of Use . . . . Tour
Towns . . . . Vernon Hills
County . . . . Lake

Author's Comments: Best designed park I've ever seen. Terrific for families for a full-day outing because of all the other recreational facilities available here. Call Vernon Hills Park District for a detailed map. Great for fledgling bikers.

Nearby trails: There is another trail (2.8 miles) directly north of Rt. 60 originating at Little Bear Lake on Lakeview Pkwy. Contact Julie Freed for detailed map. (See below) Daniel Wright Woods is southeast. Old School is northeast.

For Detailed Information
**Northeastern Illinois Planning Commission
400 West Madison St.
Chicago, IL 60606   312-454-0400**

**Julia E. Freed, Recreation Supervisor
Vernon Hills Park District
610 Cherry Valley Rd.
Vernon Hills, IL 60061-2651   708-367-7270**

For Calendar of Events
in Surrounding Communities
**Vernon Hills Village Hall
290 Evergreen Dr.
Vernon Hills, IL 60061   708-367-3700**

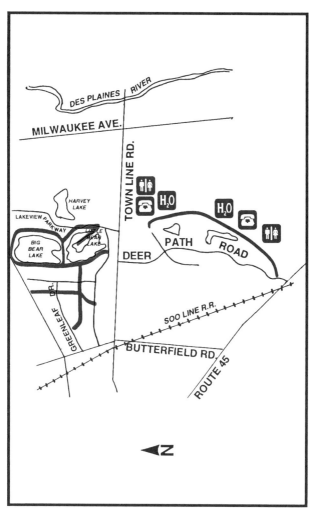

Directions for parking: Tri-State (I-94) to Rt. 60
west (Town Line Rd.). Cross Rt. 21 and go south
on DeerPath Rd. East on Cherokee Rd. and
park at the end of the road.

Zion Trail

Trail Distance . . . . 6.5 Miles
(2.5 miles on city streets)

Trail Surface . . . .
Paved and concrete sidewalk

Type of Use . . . . Tour

Towns . . . . Zion

County . . . . Lake

Author's Comments: The Western leg of this trail runs parallel to the North Shore Bike Trail on Galilee Ave. This trail is difficult to follow on Carmel Blvd. going east to Sheridan Rd. It is also difficult to follow on 17th Ave. going west to Galilee Ave. The easternmost leg, along Edina and Hillside Ave's., is nice, although I would not recommend this for a family bike ride due to the trail ambiguities and numerous street crossings.

Nearby trails: Des Plaines River to the west.

For Detailed Information
Zion Park District
2400 Dowie Memorial Dr.
Zion, IL 60090   708-746-5500

Northeastern Illinois Planning Commission
400 West Madison Street
Chicago, IL 60606   312-454-0400

For Calendar of Events
in Surrounding Communities
Zion City Hall
2828 Sheridan
Zion, IL 60099   708-872-4546

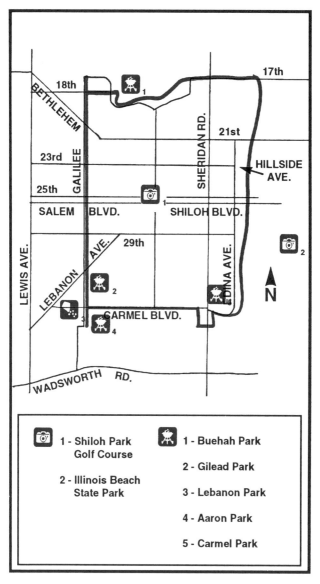

Directions for parking: Tri-State to Rt. 173 east. At Lewis Ave. crossing Rt. 173 becomes Bethlehem Ave., turning southeast. Continue southeast on Bethlehem. When Galilee intersects, turn south and park along the street.

Du Page County Trails

Blackwell Forest Preserve
Churchill Woods
Danada
Fullersburg
Green Valley Forest Preserve
Herrick Lake
Illinois Prairie Path Mid-Section
Illinois Prairie Path Northwest
Illinois Prairie Path Southwest
McDowell Grove Forest Preserve
Oak Brook Bike Path
Pratts Wayne Woods
Waterfall Glen
Wayne Grove
West Branch Reservoir
West Branch Upper
West DuPage Woods
Wood Dale Grove
York Woods

Blackwell Forest Preserve Trail

Trail Distance . . . . 8.3 Miles
Trail Surface . . . .
    Crushed limestone - main trail
        Mowed grass, wood chips -
                    cutback trails

Type of Use . . . .
                    Tour - main trail
            Mountain - cutback trails
Towns . . . . Warrenville, Winfield
County . . . . DuPage
HANDICAP FACILITIES

Author's Comments: This is a great trail for bird watching. Meadows, marshes, woods and savannas help break up the prairie around McKee Marsh. Take your bike down to Gary's Mill Rd. to see the west branch of the DuPage River. Try camping here one weekend. It's a family-oriented forest preserve.

Connecting/Nearby trails: Plans are underway for a trail connection from Blackwell to the west branch of the DuPage River Forest Preserve to the north. Plans are also underway for a Regional Trail connection from Blackwell to Herrick Lake and Danada to the southeast. The Illinois Prairie Path connects to the southeast. McDowell Grove is nearby to the south.

For Detailed Information
**Forest Preserve District of DuPage County
P.O. Box 2339, 185 Spring Ave.
Glen Ellyn, IL 60138   708-790-4900**

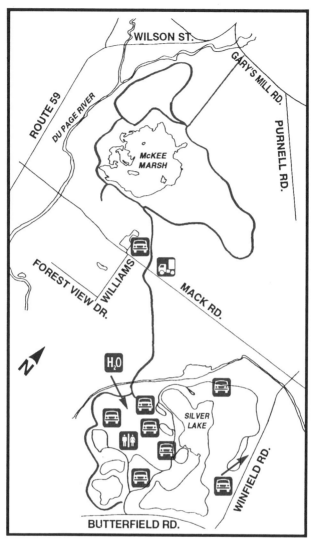

Directions for parking: Take I-355 to Rt. 56 (Butterfield Rd.). Go west 8.5 miles to the entrance on the north side of the road.

For Calendar of Events
in Surrounding Communities
Warrenfield City Hall
28 W. 630 Stafford Pl.
Warrenville, IL 60555   708-393-9427

Winfield City Hall
27 W. 465 Jewell Rd.
Winfield, IL 60190   708-665-1778

Churchill Woods Trail

Trail Distance . . . . .3.5 Miles
Trail Surface . . . . . . .Packed dirt
Type of Use . . . . .Mountain
Towns . . . .Lombard, Glen Ellyn
County . . . . .DuPage

Author's Comments: The north loop winds through prairie and woods. The surface is mostly dirt and grass. This loop is great for cross-country skiing. The road crossing east of Swift Road is not well marked. The south loop should be ridden with mountain bikes. The southwest portion has sharp turns, raspberry bushes and thistles to obstruct the trail. At one point, the trail narrows to a single lane one half foot from the water's edge. Don't let children ride the south loop unattended. The trail alongside the east branch of the DuPage River is obscured as an old unused country road. Plan on picnicking with your family at this preserve. It is analagous to a gracious, spacious house with lots of room to wander and enjoy nature's beauty.

Connecting trails: Illinois Prairie path to the south.

For Detailed Information
Forest Preserve District of DuPage County
185 Spring Ave.
Glen Ellyn, IL 60138   708-790-4900

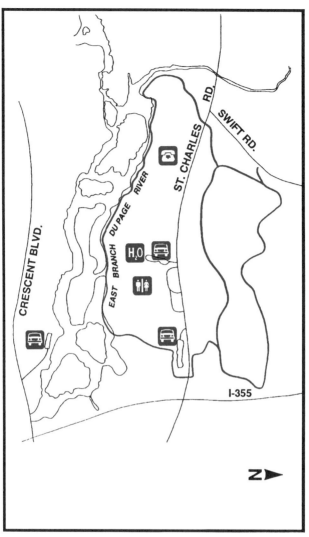

Directions for parking: Take I-290 and exit at St. Charles Rd. Go west 5.5 miles and cross Rt. 53. The entrance to the preserve is on the south side of the road.

For Calendar of Events
in Surrounding Communities
Glen Ellyn Village Hall
535 Duane
Glen Ellyn, IL 60138   708-469-5000

Lombard Civic Center
255 E. Wilson Ave.
Lombard, IL 60148   708-620-5700

Danada Trail

Trail Distance · · · · · · · · · · · 2.8 Miles
Trail Surface · · · · · · · · · · Crushed
limestone
Type of Use · · · · · · · · · · · Tour
Towns · · · · · · · · · · · · Wheaton
County · · · · · · · · · · · DuPage

Author's Comments: This trail was recently connected to Herrick Lake Forest Preserve to the west (1.4 mile connection). Make sure you remain on the regional trail when you enter the trail behind the main barn. The nature trail has been designated for walking and skiing only. If the Center is not busy, stop in at the barn and ask to see the horses. This is a meticulously maintained horse farm.

Connecting trails: Herrick Lake to the west; Illinois Prairie Path to the northwest.

For Detailed Information
**Forest Preserve District of DuPage County
P.O. Box 2339, 185 Spring Ave.
Glen Ellyn, IL 60138   708-790-4900**

For Calendar of Events
in Surrounding Communities
**Danada Equestrian Center
P.O. Box 2339
Glen Ellyn, IL 60138   708-790-4900 X 202**

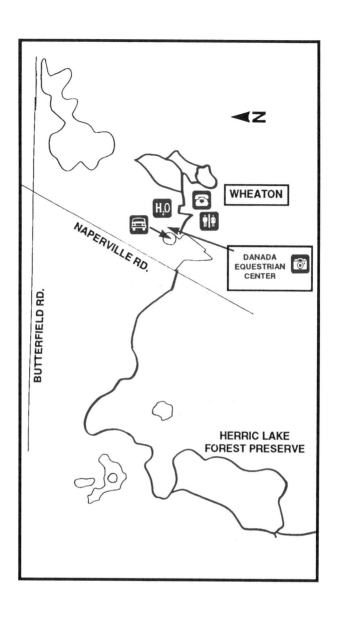

N

WHEATON

H₂O

NAPERVILLE RD.

DANADA
EQUESTRIAN
CENTER

BUTTERFIELD RD.

HERRIC LAKE
FOREST PRESERVE

Fullersburg Woods Trail

Trail Distance . . . . 3-5 Miles
Trail Surface . . . . Crushed gravel and packed dirt

Type of Use . . . . Mountain
Towns . . . . . Hinsdale, Oakbrook
County . . . . DuPage

Author's Comments: What a fun-filled day with a family! There are two trail systems. One multi-use for bikes and horses and one for walking. Make sure you stay on the trail marked for horses (on your bike). Parts of the trail have loose gravel and sand, making it tortuous on tour bikes. The labyrinth of cross trails can be confusing. I found it difficult to locate the trailhead on this trail. Follow what looks like an old dirt road. Plan on visiting the nature center. . .your kids will love the woolly mammoth exhibit. This trail is a particular favorite for cross-country skiing. It is woodsy and lush.

Connecting trails: Salt Creek Forest Preserve to the east.

For Detailed Information
Forest Preserve District of DuPage County
P.O. Box 2339, 185 Spring Ave.
Glen Ellyn, IL 60138   708-790-4900

For Calendar of Events
in Surrounding Communities
Oak Brook Village Hall
1200 Oak Brook Rd.
Oak Brook, IL 60521   708-624-2220

Hinsdale Village Hall
19 E. Chicago Ave.
Hinsdale, IL 60521   708-789-7000

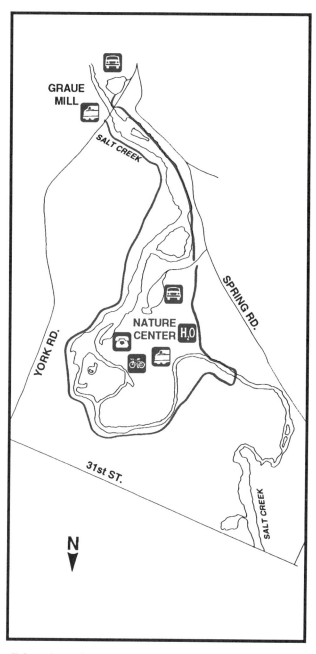

Directions for parking: Take I-294 west .5 miles
to York Rd., north .2 miles to the fork on the
left to the forest preserve entrance.

Greene Valley
Forest Preserve Trail

Trail Distance · · · · · · · · ·18 Miles

Trail Surface · · · · ·Mowed grass, packed dirt

Type of Use · · · · · · · · ·Mountain

Towns · · · · · · · · · ·Woodridge

County · · · · · · · · · ·DuPage

Author's Comments: This trail is one of my favorites because I'm so familiar with it! The first time I went on it I had my bearings wrong; hence, read the map theoretically upside down, and ended up outside the forest preserve in a stable. Not a soul in the stable knew how I arrived there. The second time I went, I took the main trail and some of the cutbacks. Take the triangle to the dog sled area. If it's not a busy day, take the road through the youth camp and explore the woods, meadows, shrubs and lowland areas. I saw deer each time I visited this trail and I also spotted a hawk and American Goldfinch.

Connecting trails: Waterfall Glen 7 miles southeast.

For Detailed Information
Forest Preserve District of DuPage County
185 Spring Ave.
Glen Ellyn, IL 60138   708-790-4900

For Calendar of Events
in Surrounding Communities
Woodridge Village Hall
1900 W. 75th
Woodridge, IL 60517   708-852-7000

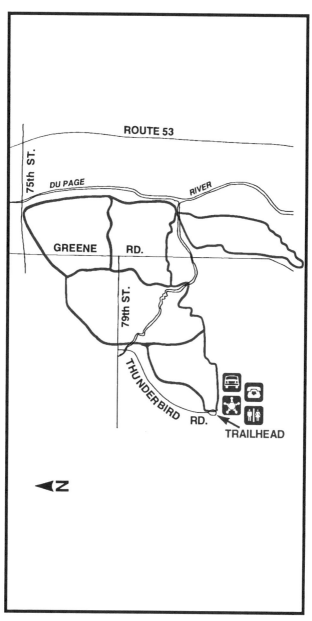

Directions for parking: Take I-55 to 53 north. Go 4.3 miles to 75th St., west one mile to Greene Rd., south .5 mile to 79th St., west .3 mile to Thunderbird Rd. south. Trail begins on the north side of the Trailhead sign. A water pump is about 100 yards into the trail on the west.

Herrick Lake Trail

Trail Distance . . . . 6 Miles
Trail Surface . . . . Crushed
limestone
Type of Use . . . . Tour, Mountain
Towns . . . . Wheaton, Warrenville
County . . . . DuPage

Author's Comments: Nicely maintained forest preserve. Meadows, forests and marshes create an environment of solitude and beauty. Try the connecting trail to Danada.

Connecting/Nearby trails: Danada is connected to Herrick on the east. Nearby trails include: Illinois Prairie Path to the north; Blackwell to the west. Plans are underway for a regional trail connection between Blackwell and Herrick Lake. Plans are also underway for a trail connection to the West Branch of the DuPage River Forest Preserve just north of Blackwell Forest Preserve. McDowell Forest Preserve is directly south.

For Detailed Information
Forest Preserve District of DuPage County
185 Spring Ave.
Glen Ellyn, IL 60138   708-790-4900

For Calendar of Events
in Surrounding Communities
Warrenville City Hall
28 W. 630 Stafford Pl.
Warrenville, IL 60555   708-393-9427

Wheaton City Hall
214 N. Wheaton
Wheaton, IL 60187   708-260-2000

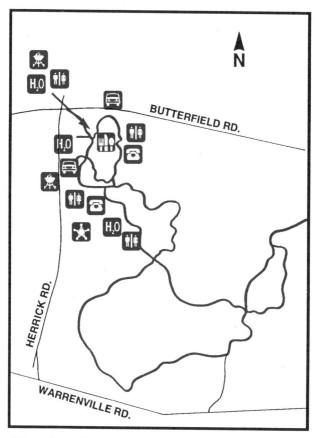

Directions for parking: Take I-88 and exit Rt. 59 north. Turn east on Butterfield Rd. (Rt. 56). Entrance is on the south side of the road. Or turn south on Herrick Rd. and enter on the east side of the road.

Illinois Prairie Path
Mid-Section
(Elmhurst to Wheaton)

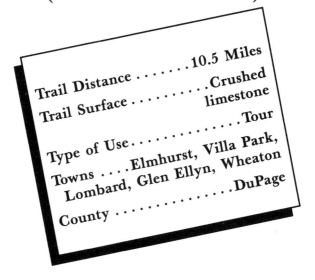

Trail Distance . . . . .10.5 Miles

Trail Surface . . . . .Crushed limestone

Type of Use . . . . .Tour

Towns . . . .Elmhurst, Villa Park, Lombard, Glen Ellyn, Wheaton

County . . . . .DuPage

Author's Comments: Here begins one of the most popular trails in the Chicago area. The Elmhurst portion is a mixture of woods and grassy parks. After crossing Salt Creek and Rt. 83 you enter Villa Park and in a few blocks pass the former home of Ovaltine (north side of the trail). At Villa Ave. the Villa Park Historical Society, housed in an old "Roarin' Elgin" commuter station, provides exhibits, rest rooms, soft drinks and trail maps (50¢). Other restored stations are located in Elmhurst and Villa Park. The trail to the west continues to be a mix of open spaces and more heavily wooded sections all the way to the DuPage River where Glen Ellyn begins. In all three "tree towns" there are numerous side street crossings which will slow you down but which are lightly traveled for the most part. This portion of the trail is popular both for its pleasant nature and ease of access. After crossing I-355 on a new bridge the trail crosses the DuPage River and proceeds uphill through a couple miles of wooded area. There is one steep descent/ascent where the former bridge is missing in Glen Ellyn. When you reach downtown Glen Ellyn you will be parallel to the Northwestern tracks. While it is a commercial area, it has an English Tudor look. There is a nice park along the trail between Glen Ellyn and Wheaton. Once you reach Main St. in Wheaton, the trail seems to disappear. Follow the street alongside the tracks for the last (or first) few blocks to the Wheaton Trailhead which is set at the end of a three story parking lot. If ice cream is a good reason to ride a bike, this trail has plenty to offer from start to finish!

Connecting trails: Illinois Prairie Path continues to the east in Berkeley and goes southwest to Aurora or northwest to Elgin from Wheaton.

See map on pages 106-107.

Directions for parking:
East Trailhead: Take I-90 to Rt. 38, west to York Rd., north 1 mile to prairie path crossing. The parking lot is on the south side behind stores.
West Trailhead: Rt. 38 to Carlton Ave., north three blocks.

For Detailed Information
NIPC
400 W. Madison St.
Chicago, IL 60606   312-454-0400

Illinois Prairie Path
P.O. Box 1085
Wheaton, IL 60189

For Calendar of Events
in Surrounding Communities
City of Elmhurst
119 Schiller
Elmhurst, IL 60126   708-530-3000

Village of Villa Park
20 S. Ardmore
Villa Park, IL 60181   708-834-8500

Glen Ellyn Village Hall
535 Duane
Glen Ellyn, IL 60137   708-469-5000

Illinois Prairie Path
Northwest Branch

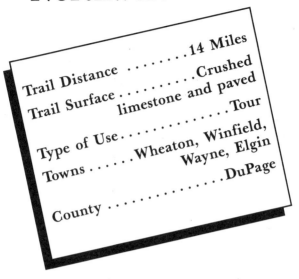

Trail Distance . . . . 14 Miles

Trail Surface . . . . Crushed limestone and paved

Type of Use . . . . Tour

Towns . . . . . . Wheaton, Winfield, Wayne, Elgin

County . . . . DuPage

Author's Comments: Despite the number of crossings, this is a nice trail. The beaver dam west of County Farm Road and Pratt's Wayne Woods provided the motivation for this author to make this trip. In October, we found ourselves riding over a variety of small snakes between Smith Rd. and Prince Crossing Rd. We wondered whether we hit a snake migration.

Connecting trails: West Branch Preserve, Pratt's Wayne Woods and Fox River Trail. Geneva Spur of Illinois Prairie Path. The connection has not yet been made to this ''spur'' out to Geneva. We took this spur from West Chicago to Geneva. The good news is that West Chicago Prairie is a wonderful sight to behold and worth the trip. The bad news is that politicians in DuPage County have approved construction efforts to expand the DuPage County Airport—which cuts into the Geneva spur. If you take this trail, expect to WALK even your mountain bike across the ruts caused by bulldozers. Write the Illinois Prairie path for a detailed map. This author does not recommend taking the Geneva Spur.

Directions for parking:
East Trailhead: Rt. 38 to Carlton Ave., north three blocks. In Wheaton, take County Farm Rd. & Geneva Rd. In Wayne, take Army Trail Rd. just east of Powis Rd.
Elgin Trailhead: Take I-90 to Rt. 25 south to Chicago St. Park in the public lots.

For Detailed Information
The Illinois Prairie Path
P.O. Box 1086
Wheaton, IL 60189

For Calendar of Events
in Surrounding Communities
Wheaton City Hall
214 N. Wheaton
Wheaton, IL 60189   708-260-2000

Winfield Village Hall
27 W. 265 Jewell Rd.
Winfield, IL 60190   708-665-1778

Wayne Village Hall
5 N. 430 Railroad
Wayne, IL 60184   708-584-3031

Elgin Area Convention &
Visitors Bureau
24 E. Chicago St.
Elgin, IL 60120   708-741-5660

Illinois Prairie Path
Southwest Branch

Trail Distance .... 13 Miles

Trail Surface .... Crushed
limestone and paved

Type of Use .... Tour

Towns ... Wheaton, Warrenville, Aurora

County .... DuPage

Author's Comments: The Illinois Prairie Path originates in Wheaton going in three directions. All mileage is measured outward from this point. This trail is the southwest portion.

To begin you will follow the sidewalk south for three blocks to Roosevelt Rd. Cross at the stoplight and pick up the trail through the woods. (Service station at corner). The next six miles provide very pleasant views of rambling homesteads and lovely woods. For a side trip, try exploring Atten Park just to the north at mile marker 2. Restrooms, water, playgrounds and more trails are available here. When you reach Batavia road in Warrenville, note two items: One, on the south side of the trail is a store with refreshments; the other is the Warrenville Grove Preserve. Ride your bikes south on Batavia Rd. about ½ mile to this delightful respite with a small waterfall on the northeast side of the road. Two miles west of Warrenville, the trail forks and you must decide whether to stay on this trail or take the Batavia spur to the Fox River Trail. I recommend you take the Batavia spur. If you continue on this trail by crossing under I-88, you will have some rough RR crossings, go through residential areas and experience an uneventful ride into Aurora.

Nearby trails: Batavia Spur and Fox River Trail (See Kane County).

See map on pages 106-107.

Directions for parking: Wheaton: Take Rt. 38 to Carlton Ave., north 3 blocks.
Warrenville: Rt. 56 to Batavia Rd., south one block. Park alongside the trail.
Aurora: Take I-88 to Farnsworth, south 1 mile to Sheffield, east to Rt. 25., half a block on the right to trail crossing.

For Detailed Information
NIPC
400 W. Madison St.
Chicago, IL 60606   312-454-0400

Illinois Prairie Path
P.O. Box 1085
Wheaton, IL 60189

For Calendar of Events
in Surrounding Communities
Wheaton City Hall
214 N. Wheaton
Wheaton, IL 60187   708-260-2000

Warrenville City Hall
28 W. 630 Stafford Pl.
Warrenville, IL 60555   708-393-9427

Greater Aurora Chamber of Commerce
Dept. K, 40 W. Downer Pl.
P.O. Box 72
Aurora, IL 60507   708-897-9214

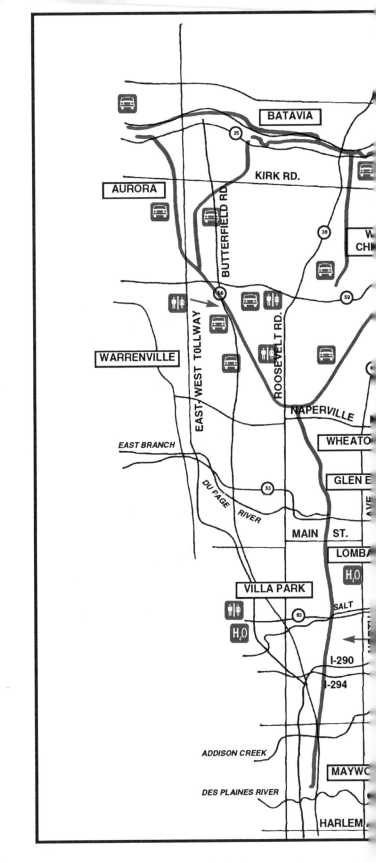

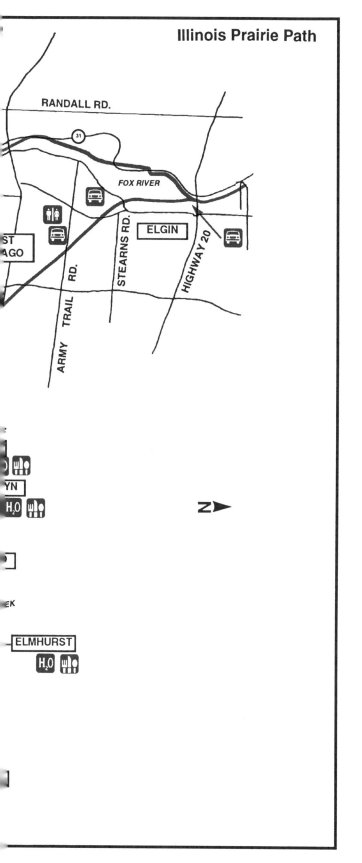

RANDALL RD.

31

FOX RIVER

ST
AGO

ELGIN

ARMY TRAIL RD.

STEARNS RD.

HIGHWAY 20

N▶

YN

ELMHURST

EK

McDowell Grove Forest Preserve Trail

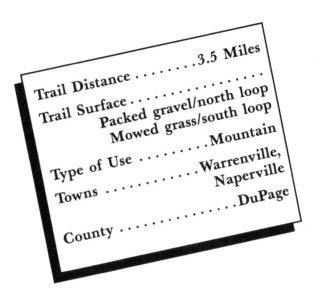

Trail Distance . . . . .3.5 Miles

Trail Surface . . . .
Packed gravel/north loop
Mowed grass/south loop

Type of Use . . . . .Mountain

Towns . . . . .Warrenville, Naperville

County . . . . .DuPage

Author's Comments: The north loop meanders around the DuPage River and Ferry Creek and is lush and green. The South loop follows the perimeter of the forest preserve boundary and is flanked by housing to the east. Be sure to follow the outward bound arrows (away from trailhead) and inward bound arrows (toward trailhead) lest you get lost as the author did.

Connecting trails: Blackwell and Illinois Prairie path to the south.

For Detailed Information
Forest Preserve District of DuPage County
P.O. Box 2339, 185 Spring Ave.
Glen Ellyn, IL 60138   708-790-4900

For Calendar of Events
in Surrounding Communities
Warrenville City Hall
28 W 630 Stratford Pl.
Warrenville, IL 60555   708-393-9427

Naperville City Hall
175 W. Jackson Ave.
Naperville, IL 60566   708-420-6111

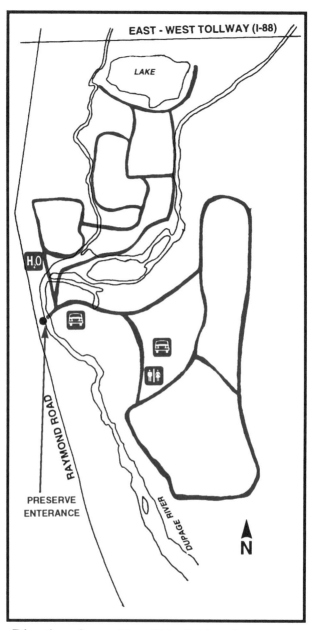

Directions for parking: Take I-88 to Rt. 59 south to McDowell Rd. east. Go south on River Rd. Entrance is on the east side of the street.

Oak Brook Bike Path

Trail Distance. . .5 Miles (approx.)
Trail Surface . . . . Blacktop
Type of Use . . . . Tour
Towns . . . . Oak Brook
County . . . . DuPage

Author's Comments: The village of Oak Brook has one of the nicest municipally developed trail systems anywhere in the area. The blacktop trails meander through the park district's extensive grounds, as well as behind McDonald's lovely headquarters grounds.

Connecting trails: Fullersburg Forest Preserve

For Detailed Information
Oak Brook Village Hall
Village Complex
1200 Oak Brook Road
(31st Street)
Spring Road
Oak Brook, IL 60521
708-990-3000

Oak Brook Park District
1300 Forest Gate Road
Oak Brook, IL 60521
708-990-4233

For Calendar of Events
in Surrounding Communities
Oak Brook Village Hall
708-990-3000

Oak Brook Park District
708-990-4233

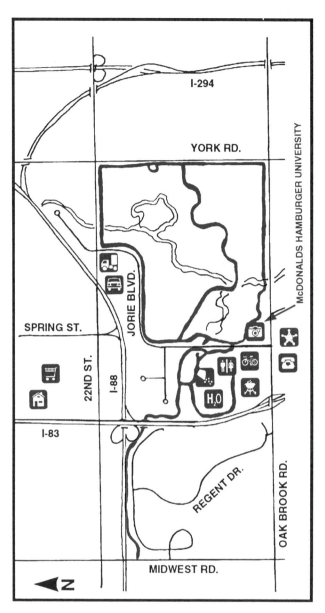

Directions for parking: Rt. 83 to 31st Street East to Jorie Blvd. North 1 block to parking on west side of street in park.

Pratts Wayne Woods Forest Preserve Trail

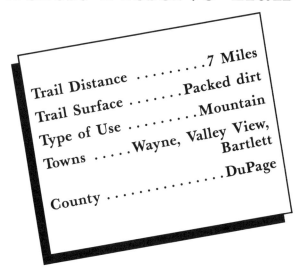

Trail Distance . . . . .7 Miles
Trail Surface . . . . . . .Packed dirt
Type of Use . . . . .Mountain
Towns . . . . .Wayne, Valley View, Bartlett
County . . . . .DuPage

Author's Comments: Use the multi-use trail. For the most part, the trails are ambiguously marked. This author got lost in the Equestrian Jump area. A general rule of thumb would be to follow what looks like a single dirt lane, especially as you approach the Illinois Prairie Path. Meadows, prairies, marshes and savannas create a varied landscape. Bring your camera if you're a bird watcher or want some great photos. This trail connects with the IPP to give you a spectacular marshlands view. I recommend you take the IPP to Powis Rd. to return to the Trailhead. This author did not ride the east loop. Please fill me in, readers.

Connecting trails: Illinois Prairie Path

For Detailed Information
Forest Preserve District of DuPage County
185 Spring Ave., P.O. Box 2339
Glen Ellyn, IL 60138   708-790-4900

For Calendar of Events
in Surrounding Communities
Wayne Village Hall
5 N 430 Railroad
Wayne, IL 60184   708-584-3031

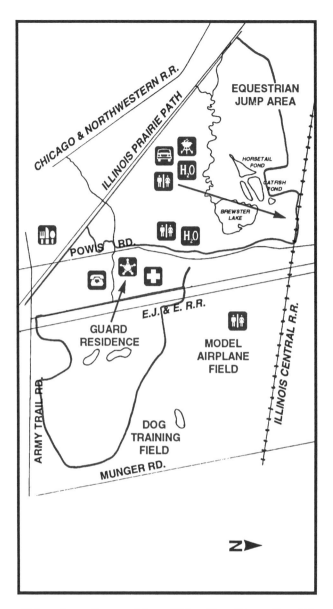

Directions for parking: Take Rt. 64 to Rt. 59, north 2.4 miles, west on Army Trail Rd. 2 miles, north on Powis Rd. ½ mile. The Park entrance is on the left and leads to the west loop. The east loop is on the right side of Powis Rd.

Waterfall Glen Forest Preserve Trail

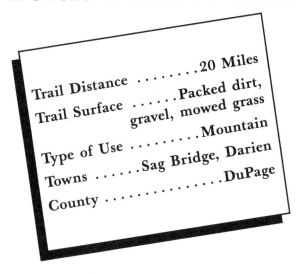

Trail Distance . . . . 20 Miles
Trail Surface . . . . . . Packed dirt, gravel, mowed grass
Type of Use . . . . Mountain
Towns . . . . . . Sag Bridge, Darien
County . . . . DuPage

Author's Comments: This trail is described as the most challenging by DuPage County Forest Preserve District. They also say this trail is the most fun. And I agree. This is yet another of my favorite trails! Plan on spending the entire day meandering from cutback to main trail. Be sure you obtain a brochure about this preserve before you visit. The history is fascinating. . .the stone for the Chicago Water Tower was quarried here. Ecosystems range from pine forests to oak groves to marshes to rocky bluffs. I don't want to spoil the surprises for you. Please don't miss this one! I can't begin to give you an adequate overview of all this trail offers. It is rough and rugged, with steep inclines, loose gravel and mowed grass. It is teaming with wildlife. I saw yearlings, beavers (including a baby beaver), and frogs galore. A species of deer I did not see is called white fallow. This park forms the perimeter boundary of Argonne National Laboratory.

For Detailed Information
**Forest Preserve District of DuPage County
P.O. Box 2339, 185 Spring Ave.
Glen Ellyn, IL 60138   708-790-4900**

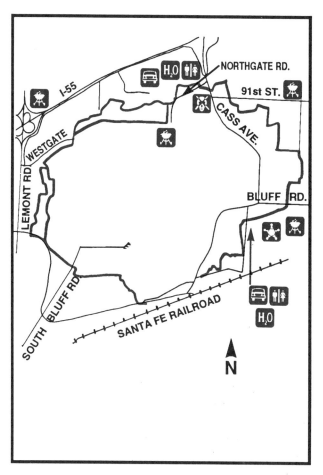

Directions for parking: I-55 exit at Cass Ave. south. For trailhead parking, turn west onto Northgate Rd., turn north to Entrance. For Education Camp parking, continue south on Cass Ave., turn east on Bluff Rd. (99th St.), turn south to the entrance.

For Calendar of Events
in Surrounding Communities
Darien City Hall
1702 Plainfield Rd.
Darien, IL 60559

Office of Public Affairs
Argonne National Laboratory
9700 South Cass Avenue
Argonne, IL 60439

Wayne Grove
Forest Preserve Trail

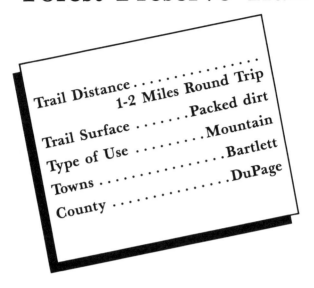

Trail Distance . . . .
1-2 Miles Round Trip

Trail Surface . . . . Packed dirt

Type of Use . . . . Mountain

Towns . . . . Bartlett

County . . . . DuPage

Author's Comments: Yes, I can imagine you are wondering why I included such a short trail. The ecosystems are so varied, from bogs to meadow to marsh to dense woods. I just loved this "little" trail. All I could think about was how beautiful and pristine it must be in the winter with snow. Horses traverse this trail. Expect ruts, rocks, and tree roots. The end of the trail spills into a Golf Course parking lot, so it's best to park at the trailhead and plan a whopping round-trip ride.

Nearby trails: Pratt's Wayne Woods to the southwest. West Branch Upper Forest Preserve to the northeast.

For Calendar of Events
in Surrounding Communities
Greater Bartlett Chamber of Commerce
Peg Mueller, Executive Director
335 S. Main
Bartlett, IL 60103   708-830-0324

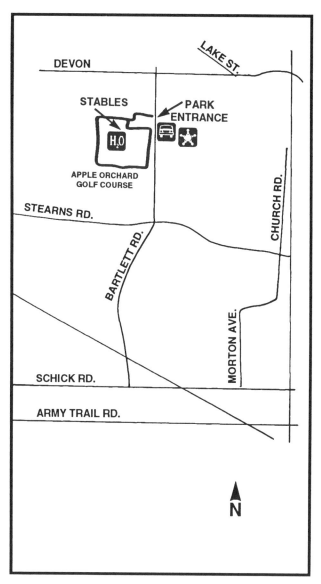

Directions for parking: Take I-355 and exit at Lake St. Go west 5.6 miles and turn left on Sterns Rd. Go 2 miles to Bartlett Rd. intersection and turn north for half a mile. Entrance on the west side of the street.

West Branch Reservoir Forest Preserve Trail

Trail Distance . . . . 1-2 Miles
Trail Surface . . . . Crushed
limestone and packed dirt
Type of Use . . . . Mountain
Towns . . . . Bartlett, Carol Stream
County . . . . DuPage
HANDICAP FACILITIES

Author's Comments: WARNING! Do not allow children under twelve to ride this one. This is probably the only dangerous trail I took in the entire Chicagoland area. The trail begins innocently enough on crushed limestone. It soon enters a wooded section that becomes an archipelago between the water-filled quarry and the West Branch of the DuPage River. The frightening portion of this trail is the archipelago that is steep, rugged, strewn with tree stumps, roots and eroded dirt sides. You can see the water at both sides of your feet on this trail. The ground varies between 1' and 5' above the water line. It reminds me of the worst roller coaster ride I could imagine. I had to extend my legs to balance while riding these hills over the water. I almost wiped out twice. Don't let your kids near this one without adult supervision. Despite the danger, it is the most exhilarating trail I've ridden.

Connecting trails: Wayne Grove Forest Preserve to the northwest; West Branch Upper Forest Preserve to the northeast; and Pratt's Wayne Forest Preserve to the west.

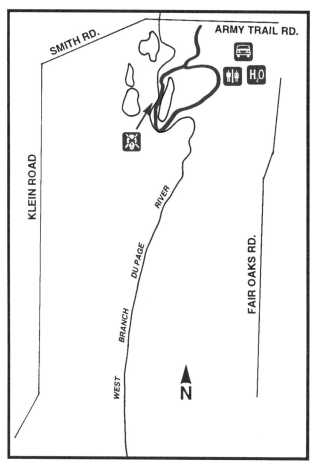

Directions for parking: I-355 to Rt. 64 (North Ave.), west 7 miles to Fair Oaks Rd., north 2 miles to Army Trail Rd., west .2 miles to entrance on the south side of the road.

*For Calendar of Events
in Surrounding Communities*
**Bartlett Village Hall
228 Main St.
Bartlett, IL 60103   708-837-0800**

**Carol Stream Village Hall
500 N. Gary Ave.
Carol Stream, IL 60188   708-665-7050**

West Branch Upper Forest Preserve Trail

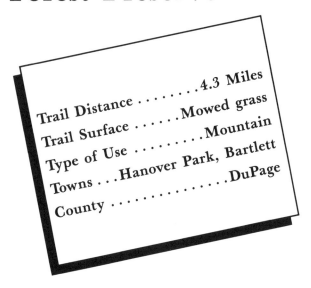

Trail Distance . . . . 4.3 Miles
Trail Surface . . . . . . Mowed grass
Type of Use . . . . Mountain
Towns . . . Hanover Park, Bartlett
County . . . . DuPage

Author's Comments: Prairie, hill, prairie, hill! What an aerobic workout! I began this trail feeling peaceful and graceful while looking at the surrounding prairies, hills and woods. My peace soon changed to boredom. Trees line the perimeter of this trail. Let me know if the eastern portion is any more interesting than the western. Trails are well marked since they are the only areas that are mowed.

Connecting trails: West Branch Reservoir to the south. Wayne Woods to the southwest.

**For Calendar of Events
in Surrounding Communities
Hanover Park Village Hall
2121 Lake
Hanover Park, IL 60103   708-837-3800**

**Bartlett Village Hall
228 Main St.
Bartlett, IL 60103   708-837-0800**

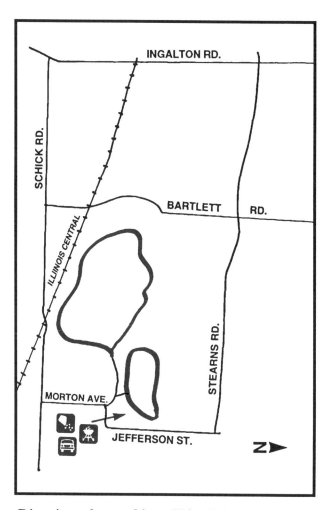

Directions for parking: Take I-355 to Rt. 64 (North Ave.), go west 5 miles to County Farm Rd. Go north 3 miles to Schick. Jog west 2 blocks, then continue north on Morton Ave. When Morton Ave. intersects with Lawrence, you have reached the Trailhead. Park on the grass on the north side of Lawrence Ave.

West DuPage Woods Forest Preserve Trail

Trail Distance . . . .
1.8 Miles - west trail
4 miles - east trail

Trail Surface . . . .
West trail -
Crushed gravel & packed dirt
East trail -
Mowed grass at Elsen's Hill

Type of Use . . . . Mountain

Towns . . . . West Chicago

County . . . . DuPage

Author's Comments:
West Trail: Rough, rugged, and mosquito-laden. This trail is lush and verdant due to its proximity to the DuPage River. Plan on getting lost as auxiliary trails confuse the ambiguously marked bike trail.

Elsen's Hill - East Trail: Elsen's Hill is a high point in DuPage County. You'll need to get off your Mountain bike to climb this one...but the view is expansive. Even with a map and trying to stay on the service road, I got lost. This is a heavily used horse trail - hoof marks and digestive remains will keep your eyes focused on the trail! Try to stop for views of the River. This is a very hilly trail which provides vistas of the Preserve. A large portion runs alongside the West Branch of the DuPage River.

Connecting trails: Blackwell Forest Preserve is located south on Rt. 59. Herrick Lake Forest Preserve is located southeast of Blackwell.

For Detailed Information
Forest Preserve District of DuPage County
P.O. Box 2339   185 Spring Ave.
Glen Ellyn, IL 60138   708-790-4900

For Calendar of Events
in Surrounding Communities
City of West Chicago • 475 Main
West Chicago, IL 60185
708-293-2200 or 708-231-3322

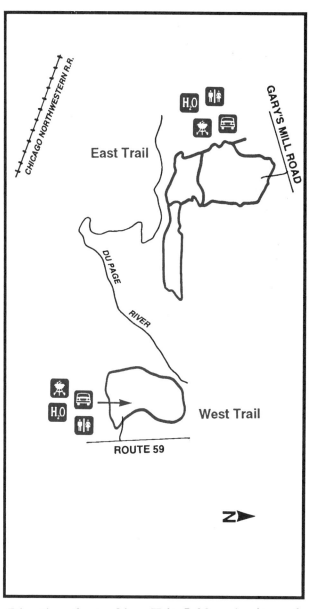

Directions for parking: Take I-88 and exit north on Rt. 59. Cross Rt. 56. For Elsen's Hill Trail, turn east on Rt. 38, then northeast on Gary's Mill Rd. Turn north for entrance. For Western Trail, take I-88 north on Rt. 59. Cross Rt. 56. After crossing Rt. 38, look for the entrance on the east side of the road.

Wood Dale Grove
Forest Preserve Trail

Trail Distance ....1.1 Miles
Trail Surface .Crushed limestone
Type of Use............Tour
Towns ..Wood Dale, Bensenville
County ....DuPage
HANDICAP FACILITIES

Author's Comments: I included this trail because of its simplicity and beauty. The trail is easy, flat and smooth. Terrific for beginning bikers or wheelchairs. The ride around the lake into the woods gives enough variety to make this a delightful outing. Bring a picnic lunch and a few youngsters while you fish, bike, and enjoy this respite.

For Detailed Information
Forest Preserve District of DuPage County
185 Spring Ave.
Glen Ellyn, IL 60138   708-790-4900

For Calendar of Events
in Surrounding Communities
Wood Dale City Hall
404 N. Wood Dale Rd.
Wood Dale, IL 60191   708-766-4900

Bensenville Village Hall
201 S. Bloomingdale Rd.
Bloomingdale, IL 60108   708-893-7000

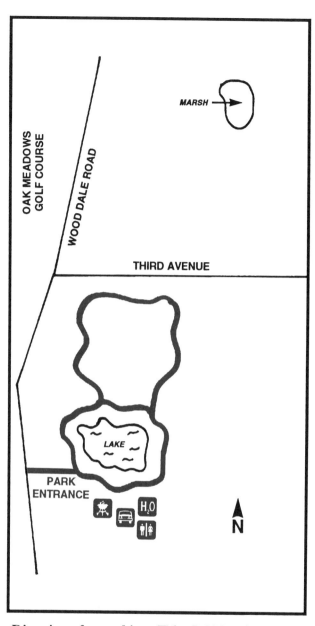

Directions for parking: Take I-290 exit at Lake St. (Rt. 20). Go north on Wood Dale Rd. and enter on the east side of the street.

York Woods Trail

Trail Distance . . . . ½–1 Mile
Trail Surface . . . . Blacktop
Type of Use . . . . Tour
Towns . . . . Oak Brook
County . . . . DuPage

Author's Comments: This is a nice little park in the midst of an otherwise busy area. The trail along Frontage Road is a little noisy, but still worth the effort — the trees are thick and lush. New bikers and handicapped individuals will enjoy the beauty and ease of this trail.

For Detailed Information
Mr. John Christiansen,
Interim ADA Coordinator
Forest Preserve District of DuPage County
185 Spring Avenue
Glen Ellyn, IL 60138
708-790-4900

For Calendar of Events
in Surrounding Communities
Oak Brook Jaycees, Inc.
P.O. Box 1138
Oak Brook, IL 60521
708-512-0405

Oak Brook Park District
1300 Forest Gate Road
Oak Brook, IL 60521
708-990-4233

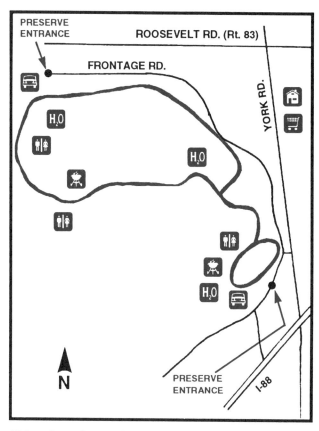

Directions for parking: Roosevelt Road (Rt. 38) to York Road to first right turn. Two locations to park.

Grundy County Trails

I & M Canal

Will County Trails

Kankakee River State Park
University Park

McHenry County Trails

Moraine Hills State Park
Prairie Trail North
Prairie Trail South

I&M Canal State Trail

Trail Distance ....55 Miles
Trail Surface .Crushed limestone
& limestone

Type of Use ....Tour, Mountain
Towns .....Channahon, Morris,
Seneca, Marseilles, Ottawa,
Utica, LaSalle/Peru

County ....Will & Grundy

Author's Comments: This trail is close enough to make a nice day trip to explore some or all of it. It is also long enough to justify spending a weekend away hiking and biking the trail and enjoying the river valley. The towns are pleasant to visit and quite a change from Chicago's suburbs. Buffalo Rock and Starved Rock State Parks are in close proximity to the trail. Buffalo Rock, which is closer to the trail but up a very steep hill, is small, yet offers a pool and beautiful view of the Illinois River. Starved Rock is across the river at Utica and also is situated atop a long uphill ride. It is noted for its miles of hiking trails through woods and stone canyons. Try the turtle specialties at the restaurants in the canal towns! Good maps are available at the ranger stations throughout the various state parks and at the Illinois Waterway Visitors Center. Be sure to pick up one for more detailed information about the trail's history.

NOTE: The I & M Canal Trail begins in Channahon and goes southwest to LaSalle/Peru. The trail does NOT CONNECT to Willow Springs I & M Canal Trail.

Nearby trails: Waterfall Glen, DuPage County

Directions for parking: Channahon: I-55 to Rt. 6, west to Canal St., south 2 blocks to Ranger Station & Campground parking (1 block more to 2nd parking lot.) Parking is available in all of the state parks and towns along the way.

For Detailed Information
Executive Director
I & M Canal NHC
30 N. Bluff St.
Joliet, IL 60435   815-740-2047

Illinois Dept. of Conservation
Office of Public Information
524 S. Second St.
Springfield, IL 62701-1787   217-782-7454

For Calendar of Events
in Surrounding Communities
Heritage Corridor Visitors Bureau
81 N. Chicago St.
Joliet, IL 60431   1-800-535-5682
or 815-727-2323

Grundy County Assn. Commerce and Ind.
Patricia G. Hibner, Exec. Dir.
112 E. Washington St.
Morris, IL 60450   815-942-0113

Illinois River Area Chamber of Commerce
Bill Steep, President
138 Washington St., P.O. Box 326
Marseilles, IL 61341   815-795-2323

Ottawa Area Chamber of Commerce and Ind.
Lawrence W. Bianchi, Exec. Dir.
100 W. Lafayette St., P.O. Box 888
Ottawa, IL 61350   815-433-0084

Illinois Valley Area Chamber of Commerce
Leonard J. Corti, Exec. Dir.
300 Bucklin St., P.O. Box 446
LaSalle, IL 61301   815-223-4827

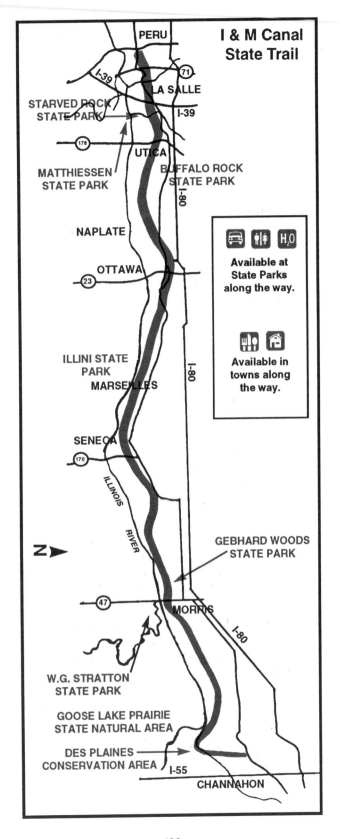

Kankakee River State Park Trail

Trail Distance ....9 Miles
Trail Surface ....
    Crushed limestone and dirt
Type of Use .... Tour, Mountain
Towns ..Kankakee, Bourbonnais
County ....Will

Author's Comments: This trail was just finished in 1993. It runs through the park and is just a short distance from the river. Most of it is fairly level and heavily wooded. About a third of the trail is through developed picnic groves in the park while the rest is in the woods. On the south side of the River, within the park boundary, are some extensive horse and hiking trails which are not posted as restricted to mountain bikes. As of this writing, park officials cannot decide whether use of bikes on these trails would be an overall benefit or detriment to the nature of the park. The trail and the park are underused treasures waiting to be explored.

For Detailed Information
Kankakee River State Park
Park Office, P.O. Box 37
Bourbonnais, IL 60914   815-933-1383

Kankakee River State Park
Canoe Trips Co. • P.O. Box 226
Bourbonnais, IL 60914   815-932-0488

Dept. of Conservation
Office of Public Information
510 Lincoln Tower Plaza
524 S. Second St.
Springfield, IL 62706   217-782-7454

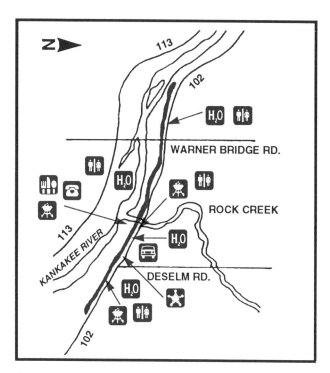

Directions for parking: I-57. A few miles south of Manteno, take the road going west to Deselm Rd. Take Deselm Road south to the Main Park Entrance.

University Park South Bikeway System

Trail Distance . . . .
4.25 Miles one way

Trail Surface . . . . Paved
and sidewalk

Type of Use . . . . Tour

Towns . . . . Park Forest South,
Chicago Heights, S. Chicago Hts.,
University Park

County . . . . Will

Author's Comments: The trail is ambiguous and unmarked between Hickory Ave. & Exchange Ave. Around the loop, it is difficult to follow with numerous sidewalks interconnecting the trail. The rolling hills and woods on Exchange Ave., west of Steger and Monee Rd., are beautiful. A paved trail takes you into Pine Lake Woods, which is a great place to fish or picnic. The Bridge at Hickory has rough cross slats. I suggest walking your bike over.

For Detailed Information
Northeastern Illinois Planning Commission
400 W. Madison
Chicago, IL 60606   312-454-0400

Village of University Park
Parks and Recreation
Village Hall - 698 Burnham Dr.
University Park, IL 60466

For Calendar of Events
in Surrounding Communities
Monee Village Hall
500 E. Court St.
Monee, IL 60449   708-534-8301

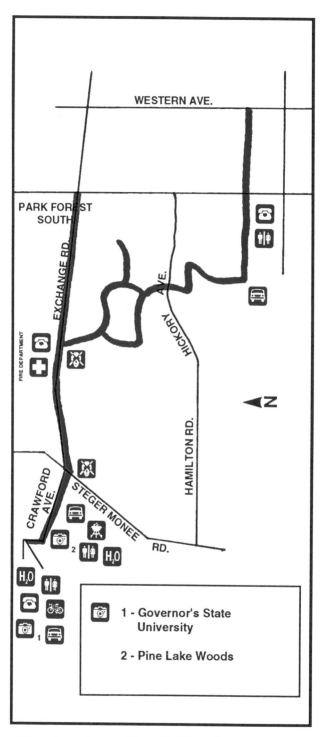

Directions for parking: I-57 to Rt. 30, east 2.5 miles to Western, south 3.5 miles to Amherst. Park on street.

Moraine Hills
State Park Trail

Trail Distance .... 10 Miles total

Trail Surface . Crushed limestone

Type of Use .... Tour, Mountain

Towns ....
    McHenry, Volo, Island Lake,
              Wauconda, Fox Lake
.....................McHenry

County .... McHenry

Author's Comments: This is a recent addition
to the State Park system. The glacial lakeland
is rolling and the trail goes in and out of wooded
areas into marsh areas or prairies and past lovely
lakes. Beware of fine gravel and sand on some
of the inclines — this is why a Mountain bike
is recommended. Don't miss the Interpretive
Area on Lake Defiance...a working beehive is
a site to behold! In addition to the bike trails,
there are foot trails through marsh areas. The
bike trails form three loops and are designated
for one way travel. This is a nice park system
and a great way to spend an entire day with your
family.

For Detailed Information
Moraine Hills State Park
914 S. River Rd.
McHenry, IL 60050   815-385-1624

For Boat Rental or Concession Information
815-385-8272

Illinois Department of Conservation
Office of Public Information
524 S. Second St.
Springfield, IL 62701-1787   217-782-7454

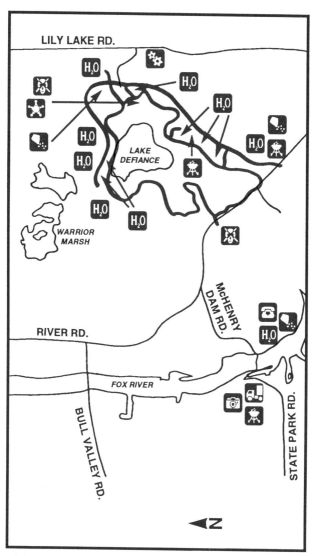

Directions for parking: Rt. 12 to 176 west or Rt. 31 to Rt. 176 east to River Road north to Park Road on right or to McHenry Dam Road on left.

For Calendar of Events
in Surrounding Communities
Wauconda Chamber of Commerce
213 S. Main St.
Wauconda, IL 60084   815-526-5580

McHenry Township
1111 N. Green St.
McHenry, IL 60050   815-385-8500

Prairie Trail - North

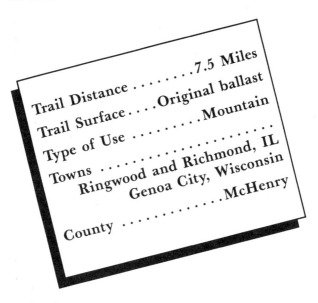

Trail Distance . . . . 7.5 Miles
Trail Surface . . . . Original ballast
Type of Use . . . . Mountain
Towns . . . . . . Ringwood and Richmond, IL
Genoa City, Wisconsin
County . . . . McHenry

Author's Comments: This trail runs along a converted C&NWRR track and ends on the Wisconsin line.

The surface is what is left of the old road bed and is pretty rough. This part of the state is rolling pasture land and wooded. A quick side trip to McHenry County's Glacial Park Woods is well worth the short ½ mile ride. The park has about 8 miles of hiking trails (closed to mountain bikes), picnic & rest room facilities, and a barn exhibit. The town of Richmond is full of antique shops and has some nice old victorian homes. The trail is quite a distance from most of Chicago and its suburbs, but might be worth the trip if you want to make a day excursion into the country to enjoy the outdoors.

For Detailed Information
Steve Weller, Manager
Planning and Development
McHenry County Conservation District
6512 Harts Rd.
Ringwood, IL 60072   815-678-4431

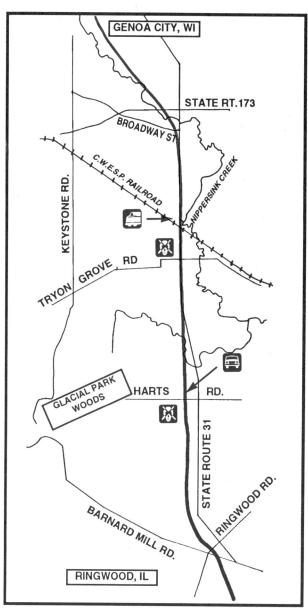

Directions for parking:
I-90 to Rt. 31 north to Ringwood. Trail begins south of Ringwood Rd. and Barnard Mill Rd. intersection.

Prairie Trail - South

Trail Distance ....5 Miles
Trail Surface ....Paved
Type of Use ....Tour, Mountain
Towns .....Crystal Lake, Algonquin
County ....McHenry

Author's Comments: A converted C&NWRR track, this is a recent addition to the Fox River Trail from Algonquin to Crystal Lake. One portion goes through and around a large sand and gravel mining area. There are also some pleasant miles through quiet residential areas, and lots of open areas. If you are pushing for miles, the surface is good and there are few cross streets to slow you down.

Connecting trails: You could start at Crystal Lake and go as far south as Aurora (see Fox River Trail) or as far east as Hillside (see Prairie Path NW. and E.) and spend the whole time on improved paths, except for short detours in Elgin and Batavia. McHenry County will be making a connection between this trail and the Prairie Trail North within the next few years. In the meantime, if you ride a mountain bike try the Prairie Trail North.

For Detailed Information
Steve Weller, Manager
McHenry County Conservation District
6512 Harts Rd.
Ringwood, IL 60072   815-678-4431

Rails to Trails Conservancy
1400 Sixteenth St., NW
Washington, DC 20036

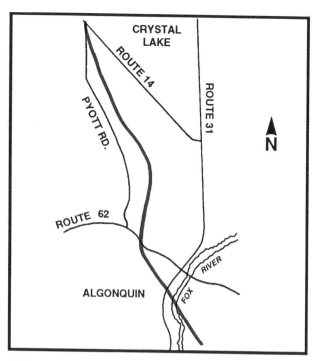

Directions for parking:
Crystal Lake:
(1) I-90 west (NW Tollway) to Rt. 31 north. Turn northwest on Rt. 14 (Virginia Cut-Off Rd.) Pyott Rd. intersects from the south. Park in southeast segment where Pyott Rd. and Rt. 14 intersect. (2) Rt. 31 south (Northwest Hwy.) to Rt. 14 west. Pass Pingree Rd., turn south on Pyott Rd. Where Pyott Rd. and Rt. 14 intersect, park in southeast segment.
Algonquin: I-90 west to Rt. 31 north to Rt. 62 west about a mile. Park alongside road east of Pyott Rd.

*For Calendar of Events
in Surrounding Communities*
**Greater Crystal Lake Area
Chamber of Commerce
427 Virginia St.
Crystal Lake, IL 60014   815-459-1300**

**Algonquin Village Hall
2 S. Main St.
Algonquin, IL 60102   815-658-3244**

ILLINOIS CYCLING ASSOCIATIONS AND CLUB DIRECTORY

ASSOCIATIONS

Chicagoland Bicycle Federation, Chicago
312-42-PEDAL

Illinois Cycling Association, Northbrook
708-498-2309

League of American Wheelmen, Buffalo Grove
708-459-8242

Rails-to-Trails Conservancy, Springfield
217-789-4782

CLUBS

Active Endeavors, Evanston
708-869-7070

Alberto's Sport, Winnetka
708-446-2042

Arlington Road Club, Elk Grove
708-893-0097

Belmont Race Club, Chicago
312-461-0122

Bike Club of Lake County, Libertyville
708-450-8227

Bike Psychos, Oak Lawn
312-239-8772

Bithead Velo, LaGrange
312-938-3522

Blackhawk Bicycle Club, Rockford
815-332-4195

Blue Horizon Wheelmen, Wheaton
708-665-6896

Byrons Bicycle Club, Glenwood
708-758-4500

Chi-Town Golden Wheels, Darien
708-986-1463

DeKalb County Bicycle Club
815-758-8879

Elmhurst Bicycle Club, Elmhurst
708-530-BIKE

Evanston Bicycle Club, Evanston
708-866-7743

Flyer Bicycle Club, Naperville
708-979-6765

Folks on Spokes, Homewood
708-730-5179

Great Plains Racing Team, Bartlett
708-213-8589

GSLAM, Northfield
708-441-5051

Joliet Bicycle Club, Joliet
815-436-3539

McHenry County Bicycle Club, Crystal Lake
815-337-5996

Midwest Masters Cycling Team, Libertyville
708-816-8778

Mount Prospect Bike Club, Mount Prospect
708-439-9830

Naperville Bicycle Club, Naperville
708-357-9000 x616

Northbrook Bicycle Club, Northbrook
708-205-0429

Oak Park Cycle Club, Oak Park
312-440-6163

Penguin Bicycle Club, Chicago
312-281-3444

Redline, Elk Grove
708-439-3340

Second City Cyclists, Chicago
312-465-1051

South Chicago Wheelmen, Crete
708-672-9066

Strada Velosport, Westchester
708-531-9059

Straight Up Cycling Club, Yorkville
708-553-0021

Team Apache, Berwyn
708-788-1674

Team Illinois Racing, Glencoe
708-835-4388

Turin Bicycling Society, Evanston
708-864-3848

Univ. of Chicago Velo Club, Chicago
312-684-6553

Velo Club Roubaix, Highland Park
312-444-9355

West Suburban Wheelmen, Elmhurst
708-834-4290

Wheeling Wheelmen, Wheeling
708-516-1817

Windy City Wheelmen, Chicago
312-282-6029

Information courtesy of the
Chicago Area Bicycle Dealers Association.